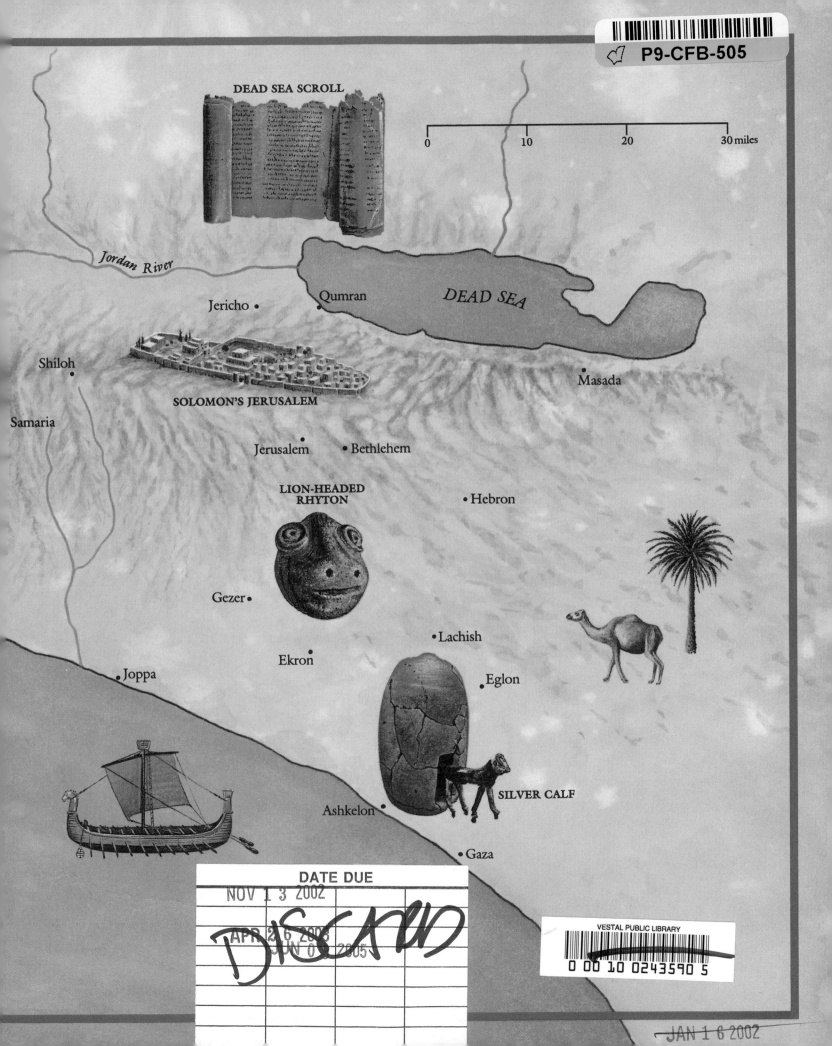

DEAD SEA SCROLL

0   10   20   30 miles

Jordan River

Jericho •   • Qumran   DEAD SEA

Shiloh •

SOLOMON'S JERUSALEM

Samaria   • Masada

Jerusalem •   • Bethlehem

LION-HEADED
RHYTON   • Hebron

Gezer •

Ekron •   • Lachish

Joppa •   • Eglon

                    SILVER CALF

Ashkelon •

• Gaza

THE
HOLY LAND

TIME-LIFE BOOKS

EDITOR-IN-CHIEF: Thomas H. Flaherty
Director of Editorial Resources: Elise D. Ritter-Clough
Executive Art Director: Ellen Robling
Director of Photography and Research: John Conrad Weiser
Editorial Board: Dale M. Brown, Janet Cave, Roberta Conlan, Robert Doyle, Laura Foreman, Jim Hicks, Rita Thievon Mullin, Henry Woodhead
Assistant Director of Editorial Resources: Norma E. Shaw

PRESIDENT: John D. Hall

Vice President and Director of Marketing: Nancy K. Jones
Editorial Director: Russell B. Adams, Jr.
Director of Production Services: Robert N. Carr
Production Manager: Prudence G. Harris
Director of Technology: Eileen Bradley
Supervisor of Quality Control: James King

Editorial Operations
Production: Celia Beattie
Library: Louise D. Forstall
Computer Composition: Deborah G. Tait (Manager), Monika D. Thayer, Janet Barnes Syring, Lillian Daniels
Interactive Media Specialist: Patti H. Cass

Time-Life Books is a division of Time Life Incorporated

PRESIDENT AND CEO: John M. Fahey, Jr.

Library of Congress Cataloging in Publication Data
The Holy Land / by the editors of Time-Life Books.
    p. cm.—(Lost civilizations)
Includes bibliographical references and index.
ISBN 0-8094-9866-9 (trade)
ISBN 0-8094-9867-7 (lib. bdg.)
1. Palestine—Antiquities.
2. Bible—Antiquities.
3. Excavations (Archaeology)—Palestine.
4. Palestine—History—To AD 70.
I. Time-Life Books. II. Series.
DS111.H65   1992
933—dc20   92-11160

LOST CIVILIZATIONS

SERIES EDITOR: Dale M. Brown
Administrative Editor: Philip Brandt George

Editorial staff for: *The Holy Land*
Art Director: Susan K. White
Picture Editor: Kristin Baker Hanneman
Text Editors: Robert Somerville (principal), Charlotte Anker
Associate Editor/Research: Jacqueline L. Shaffer
Assistant Editors/Research: Constance Contreras, Katherine L. Griffin
Assistant Art Director: Bill McKenney
Senior Copyeditor: Anne Farr
Picture Coordinator: Gail Feinberg
Editorial Assistant: Patricia D. Whiteford

Special Contributors: Windsor Chorlton, George Constable, Marge duMond, Ellen Galford, Alan Lothian, Barbara Mallen, Roberta Maltese, Daniel Stashower, David S. Thomson (text); Vilasini Balakrishnan, Jocelyn G. Lindsay, Mary Grace Mayberry, Gail Prensky, Evelyn Prettyman (research); Roy Nanovic (index)

Correspondents: Elisabeth Kraemer-Singh (Bonn), Christine Hinze (London), Christina Lieberman (New York), Maria Vincenza Aloisi (Paris), Ann Natanson (Rome). Valuable assistance was also provided by: Nihal Tamraz (Cairo); Marlin Levin (Jerusalem); Judy Aspinall (London); Elizabeth Brown, Katheryn White (New York); Leonora Dodsworth (Rome); Traudl Lessing (Vienna)

The Consultants:
William G. Dever, PhD, is chairman of the Department of Near Eastern Studies at the University of Arizona. An archaeologist in the Near East for nearly 30 years, he is a world-renowned expert in biblical archaeology.

Joe D. Seger, ThD, is Middle Eastern Archaeologist and professor of religion and anthropology at Mississippi State University, where he is director of the Cobb Institute of Archaeology. Over the past 25 years he has participated in extensive excavations in the Holy Land and has published widely in the field.

James F. Strange, PhD, chair of the Department of Religious Studies at the University of South Florida, reviewed material relating to the archaeology of the New Testament.

Kenneth Holum, PhD, professor of history at the University of Maryland, is director of the Combined Caesarea Expeditions. Widely published in the field, he consulted on text and pictures dealing with the Herodian era.

James C. VanderKam, PhD, is professor of theology at the University of Notre Dame. A specialist in Hebrew Scriptures, he reviewed the section dealing with the Dead Sea Scrolls.

Other Publications:

WEIGHT WATCHERS® SMART CHOICE RECIPE COLLECTION
TRUE CRIME
THE AMERICAN INDIANS
THE ART OF WOODWORKING
ECHOES OF GLORY
THE NEW FACE OF WAR
HOW THINGS WORK
WINGS OF WAR
CREATIVE EVERYDAY COOKING
COLLECTOR'S LIBRARY OF THE UNKNOWN
CLASSICS OF WORLD WAR II
TIME-LIFE LIBRARY OF CURIOUS AND UNUSUAL FACTS
AMERICAN COUNTRY
VOYAGE THROUGH THE UNIVERSE
THE THIRD REICH
THE TIME-LIFE GARDENER'S GUIDE
MYSTERIES OF THE UNKNOWN
TIME FRAME
FIX IT YOURSELF
FITNESS, HEALTH & NUTRITION
SUCCESSFUL PARENTING
HEALTHY HOME COOKING
UNDERSTANDING COMPUTERS
LIBRARY OF NATIONS
THE ENCHANTED WORLD
THE KODAK LIBRARY OF CREATIVE PHOTOGRAPHY
GREAT MEALS IN MINUTES
THE CIVIL WAR
PLANET EARTH
COLLECTOR'S LIBRARY OF THE CIVIL WAR
THE EPIC OF FLIGHT
THE GOOD COOK
WORLD WAR II
HOME REPAIR AND IMPROVEMENT
THE OLD WEST

For information on and a full description of any of the Time-Life Books series listed above, please call 1-800-621-7026 or write:
Reader Information
Time-Life Customer Service
P.O. Box C-32068
Richmond, Virginia 23261-2068

This volume is one in a series that explores the worlds of the past, using the finds of archaeologists and other scientists to bring ancient peoples and their cultures vividly to life.

Other volumes include:

Egypt: Land of the Pharaohs
Aztecs: Reign of Blood & Splendor
Pompeii: The Vanished City
Incas: Lords of Gold and Glory
Mound Builders and Cliff Dwellers
Wondrous Realms of the Aegean
The Magnificent Maya
Sumer: Cities of Eden

The dates used in this book are at times approximate, based on the informed guesses of historians and archaeologists.

THE
HOLY LAND

By the Editors of Time-Life Books

TIME-LIFE BOOKS, ALEXANDRIA, VIRGINIA

CONTENTS

ONE
TERRAIN AND TESTAMENT: DIGGING FOR THE BIBLE
13

ESSAY: A Painter's Pilgrimage   38

TWO
CITIES OF THE PROMISED LAND
49

ESSAY: The Many Ages of Ashkelon   75

THREE
JERUSALEM: THE DREAM AND THE NIGHTMARE
85

ESSAY: The Treasures of Qumran   109

FOUR
IN THE FOOTSTEPS OF JESUS
119

ESSAY: Herod: The Master Builder   144

Timeline 158
Acknowledgments 160
Picture Credits 160
Bibliography 161
Index 164

THE JUDEAN DESERT

*H*e turneth rivers into a
wilderness, and the watersprings into
dry ground; a fruitful land into
barrenness, for the wickedness of them
that dwell therein.

PSALM 107:33-34

GALILEE

*S*ing *praise upon the harp unto our God: Who covereth the heaven with clouds, who prepareth rain for the earth, who maketh grass to grow upon the mountains.*

PSALM 147:7-8

THE DEAD SEA

If I take the wings of the morning, and dwell in the uttermost parts of the sea; even there shall thy hand lead me, and thy right hand shall hold me.

PSALM 139:9-10

TERRAIN
AND TESTAMENT:
DIGGING
FOR THE
BIBLE

For the archaeologists at work on the western shoulder of Israel's Valley of Hinnom in 1979, the long-ago world of the Bible had an almost palpable presence. Just to the west was a ravine described in the Book of Joshua as marking the border between the territories of Judah and Benjamin, 2 of the 12 sons of the patriarch Jacob, whom God called Israel. Right next to the site ran an ancient road—known even before the Israelites first appeared in the area around the 13th century BC—that led to Bethlehem, the little town named in the Gospels as the birthplace of Jesus. And across the valley to the east lay Jerusalem, cherished center of faith since the days of King David, who had made it the Israelite capital in the 10th century BC. David's son Solomon had raised a great temple there of cedar, olive wood, gold, and bronze, saying to the Lord, "I have surely built thee an house to dwell in, a settled place for thee to abide in for ever." The temple was long gone, but in the early morning light, as the sun rose over the holy city, this place and everything around it inevitably drew the mind into the deeps of time—deeps that were about to cast up a spiritual treasure.

The Hinnom valley site was known to be an old burial ground, but, as the project leader, the Israeli archaeologist Gabriel Barkay of Tel Aviv University, said, "After 120 years of great archaeologists digging in Jerusalem, you don't expect to find much."

The oldest known biblical text—from the late seventh century BC—came to light on this tiny silver scroll, found beside the bones of ancient generations in the rock-hewn burial caves of Jerusalem's Valley of Hinnom.

Nevertheless, after working through the debris left by quarrying the hill for limestone, the excavators came upon nine burial caves that had been carved out of the rock more than 2,600 years ago, at a time when Solomon's Temple still stood. The tombs appeared to have been looted, but to the team's astonishment, one of the caves whose roof had collapsed had not been touched in all the intervening centuries. It contained the remains of nearly 100 people and a vast array of burial gifts, from pottery and glass vessels to jewelry. The greatest prizes at first seemed relatively modest: two small, rolled-up silver scrolls, evidently intended to be worn around the neck as amulets.

Dirty, cracked, and corroded, the miniature scrolls were so fragile that no attempt was made to unroll them for three years. Finally, in 1983, the director of the Israel Museum laboratory came up with a plan. First, he rinsed the amulets in a solution of alkaline salt and formic acid to remove the corrosion. Next, he coated them with an acrylic emulsion that was transparent and elastic when dried. Prevented from cracking by this see-through film, the outer layer was slowly unfurled. Then more emulsion was added to support successive layers as the unrolling continued. The process took several months, but all the care and effort brought a stunning reward.

On one of the sheets of silver, a museum specialist could make out four Hebrew characters, delicately etched in a script that had been used in the seventh century BC. These characters, *yod-he-waw-he,* were the formulation known as the Tetragrammaton—the name of God, written in consonants only and at one time deemed too sacred to say aloud. Its original pronunciation having been lost, the writers of the King James version of the Bible in 17th-century England used "Jehovah" as a guess; modern linguists consider "Yahweh" to be a closer approximation. In any event, its appearance on the tiny scroll marked a first: Never before had this holiest of Hebrew names been found on an archaeological object from Jerusalem.

There was more to come. Painstaking study of faint scratches on the scrolls revealed that they were verses from the sixth chapter of Numbers. Since the oldest previously known copy of biblical text, the Dead Sea Scrolls, dates from only as early as 150 BC, this discovery pushed the physical record of Scripture back about 450 years—perhaps to within a generation of when this particular Old Testament book was first compiled. The words themselves are as familiar now as they apparently were in that distant age: "The Lord bless thee, and keep thee: The Lord make his face shine upon thee, and be gracious

A deep cleft southwest of Jerusalem, the Valley of Hinnom served as the city's main cemetery in biblical times. Also called the Valley of the Slaughter in the Book of Jeremiah because of child sacrifices conducted there, it eventually became synonymous with hell.

unto thee: The Lord lift up his countenance upon thee, and give thee peace." Christians know them as a benediction or as a baptismal prayer. To the Jewish Barkay, the passage was particularly moving: "It is the text my father used to bless me with when I was a boy. It is found today in every Jewish prayer book. I was not digging for my roots. But you cannot help but be touched by the thought of people uttering the same verses in the same city for 2,600 years."

The spiritual dimension clearly accounts for the unique position accorded the Holy Land among the world's archaeological hunting grounds. Stretching from the rolling hills of Galilee in the north to the tortured peaks and gullies of the Judean and Negev deserts in the south, from the blue waters of the Mediterranean Sea to the bleak expanses of the Syrian Desert, this small patch of rugged landscape never achieved the sort of imperial or economic greatness enjoyed by such civilizations as those of Egypt and Greece. But in the realm of the spirit, it was a giant—the source and stage of one of the greatest of all human documents. Its enduring fascination lies not in marble statuary or dazzling palaces but in its contribution to the belief in one God—to the faith of the Jews as expressed in the books of the Old Testament, to the convictions of Christians as shaped by the additional books of the New Testament, and to Islam, which sees Muhammad as the final prophet in the line that began with Abraham.

The links between religion and archaeology are admittedly controversial. Some archaeologists view the Bible as a distorting lens and would prefer to ignore it in their investigations of the Holy Land, focusing instead on daily life, trade, technology, and other such secular matters. Others go to the opposite extreme, insisting that the whole point of digging in the Holy Land is to better comprehend the Old and New Testaments, and to confirm their historical validity. In the 1930s, the illustrious American archaeologist William Albright pronounced the search for the factual basis of Scripture an unalloyed success. "Discovery after discovery," he wrote, "has established the accuracy of innumerable details, and has brought increased recognition of the value of the Bible as a source of history."

Many modern investigators would argue the point, or at least qualify it. But most feel comfortable in a middle ground between the secular and the sacred—mindful of the Bible as they go about their work, motivated by its place in human history, but intrigued too by aspects of the Holy Land that lie beyond the bounds of the scriptural narrative.

The larger story begins far back in time. The region was actually part of the so-called Fertile Crescent, an arc of cultivable land that stretched from Mesopotamia through Upper Syria and then south along the coastal plain beside the Mediterranean as far as Egypt. Throughout the area, humans first sowed crops and raised animals for food as early as 10,000 years ago. In the course of the next few millennia, civilization itself blossomed at either end of the crescent as Egypt and Mesopotamia developed cities, extensive trade networks, and such potent new mind tools as writing and mathematics. The locale now encompassed by modern Israel, at the crossroads of these civilizations, also took part in this first flowering. Jericho, situated just north and west of the Dead Sea, was one of the world's earliest fixed settlements; a massive stone tower discovered there ranks as the oldest known example of monumental architecture.

Despite such intriguing glimpses from prehistory, students of the Holy Land seem time and again drawn to a later period, to the sweep of centuries from about the 13th century BC up to the Christian era. It was a time of almost nonstop turbulence, much of it vividly recorded in the narrative portions of the Old Testament. Almost alone among ancient national histories, the Bible recounts defeats as well as victories—and for the Israelites there were many defeats. Buffeted and bludgeoned by the great empires of the Near East, they lost large chunks of territory in wars, witnessed the destruction of their holiest shrine—the Temple built by Solomon—and saw their leaders driven into exile. Later they were ruled by the successors to Alexander the Great, then by the Romans. But through all these trials, they never ceased to believe that God had made a covenant with them, guaranteeing full and perpetual ownership of their land if they were faithful to him and obeyed his laws as spelled out in the books of Exodus, Leviticus, and Deuteronomy.

The Bible takes the story only so far, referring only indirectly to what was the final calamity for the ancient Jews. In the first century AD, they rebelled against Rome but were brutally crushed. Jerusalem and its rebuilt Temple were destroyed in AD 70, and many other communities were razed. After another abortive revolt in 135, the Roman emperor Hadrian moved to eradicate Jewish claims to this part of his empire once and for all by changing the names of cities and towns. Jerusalem became Aelia Capitolina and was dedicated to Jupiter; Jews were forbidden to set foot there except on the anniversary of the city's destruction when—legend has it—they were allowed to mourn at the site of the Temple. The province name of Judea was replaced by "Palestine"—an intentional insult, as it derived from the Greek word for the Philistines, a people who had competed with the Israelites for these fields and hills 1,000 years earlier.

In the centuries that followed, as Rome slid toward its own disaster, a new religion rose to prominence. Founded on the life and teachings of Jesus of Nazareth, it steadily gained converts throughout the Roman world—some of them in the highest of places. In AD 324, a general named Constantine became emperor and made Christianity the state religion. With this step Palestine, long viewed as an irritant among imperial territories, became sacred ground in an official sense. But it was more than just a location on a map. Its physical reality offered a link with the time when Jesus preached, as well as with the earlier epochs of the patriarchs and the prophets. Many of the faithful sought to go there, to stand where Jesus had stood, to walk in Jerusalem (whose name had been restored), to take in the whole landscape that had formed an arena for the dramas of the Old Testament. The more intimate and explicit the connection between particular places and the events related in holy texts, the better.

Identifying those connections became a passion for Constantine's devout mother, the empress Helena. She gathered up a company of monks and bishops and traveled to the Holy Land, determined to find the precise spots where Jesus was born, where he had been crucified, and where his body had been entombed before the Resurrection. When Constantine received word that she had succeeded in this venture (with divine help, she declared), he ordered each of the sites commemorated with a grand basilica. Churches, chapels, monasteries, and convents soon followed at other locations associated with the life of Jesus. Pilgrims came in ever greater numbers, retracing the footsteps of the Master in Galilee or in the Judean Desert, praying where they had been told the baby Jesus had lain in a manger at Bethlehem, worshiping along the route he had supposedly taken through the streets of Jerusalem to Calvary.

Despite the influx of Christians, control of Palestine was far from settled. Islamic armies overran the area in AD 638, and they soon developed strong religious attachments to their new territory. On the height in Jerusalem where the Jewish Temple once stood, the Muslims built a mosque and a shrine that became one of their holiest sites—the Dome of the Rock, memorializing the place where, according to the Koran, Muhammad had ascended to heaven one night to see the face of Allah. Beginning in the 11th century and continuing through the 13th, the Christian West tried to reclaim the Holy Land in a series of crusades by knights, peasants, and, on one catastrophic occasion, even children, but these bids proved futile. As Islamic control solidified, passing to the Ottoman Turks in the 16th century, Christian pilgrimage grew more difficult and dangerous, although some access to shrines was always permitted, and monasteries and convents remained, as one writer put it, "tiny islands in a hostile sea."

The Jews also had maintained a presence in Palestine all through this time. Significant portions of the Talmud, the great

For 800 years of the early Church's history, the devout looked to relics of Jesus, Mary, the disciples, and other religious figures, including saints, as a means not just of embellishing their faith but of eliciting cures and protecting themselves from evil spirits. Pilgrims and Crusaders both, on their extended journeys to the Holy Land, invariably returned to Europe with religious items they believed had supernatural powers. Nothing seemed too inconsequential to them so long as it had a religious connection; thus even dust from the Church of the Holy Sepulcher, built over Jesus' alleged tomb, was worthy of veneration. Likewise, consecrated oil from the Holy Land, kept in little silver bottles like the seventh-century AD example at right, became a substance to cherish, suitable for one imporant personage to present to another.

As the veneration of holy objects grew, so did the passion for obtaining them. In Jerusalem in AD 385, guards had to be posted around the reputed cross on which Jesus died to prevent the pilgrims who kissed it from biting off splinters to take back home with them. Because relics had a value far greater than gold, they were coveted and sometimes seized unscrupulously. When Constantinople fell to the Crusaders in AD 1204, this eastern center of Christian orthodoxy—which had built up large collections of early relics—was ransacked. And in Jerusalem, Orthodox priests were tortured to

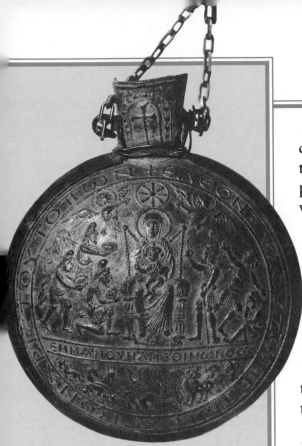

make them reveal where pieces of the true cross lay hidden.

Some churches amassed hundreds of relics. It seemed to bother few that there were frauds among them. In addition to the heads of Peter and Paul, Rome's Lateran basilica dared boast that it possessed the Tablets of Moses, the Ark of the Covenant, Aaron's rod, an urn filled with manna, a tunic belonging to Mary, the hair shirt worn by John the Baptist, and fish and loaves from the Feeding of the Five Thousand, as well as the table on which the Last Supper was served. And the chapel of Saint Lawrence, close by the Lateran Palace, claimed the umbilical cord and the foreskin of the baby Jesus. The craze for relics had plainly gotten out of hand. Duplications abounded; no fewer than three heads of John the Baptist were known to exist. Only in the 13th century, when the Eucharist and its powerful symbolism became central to Christian faith, did the obsession with relics subside.

compilation of Jewish law and customs, were composed there during the period from the third to the seventh century. But for the most part, the Jewish people were scattered far and wide throughout the world, and in any event they lacked the political wherewithal to mount organized efforts to take back their native land. But wherever they were, they continued to represent a direct, living link with biblical times, preserving the customs and beliefs of their ancestors, reciting the same prayers, celebrating the same festivals, maintaining the same unwavering respect for the law—this last perhaps their greatest legacy. And their hearts never ceased to yearn for the time when they could reclaim their heritage in a more physical sense. Every year, during Passover, which commemorated their deliverance from Egypt in the time of Moses, they would end the ceremonies with the words, "Next year in Jerusalem."

As for the Christian world, the invention of the printing press in the 15th century and the subsequent translation of the Bible from Hebrew, Greek, and Latin versions into the vernacular set the stage for renewed interest in the Holy Land. As the old stories gained a vastly wider audience, the release of new religious energies throughout Europe—spurred on by the Protestant Reformation—urged the imagination of the faithful back toward the biblical terrain.

But even for the most devoted readers, Scripture could be frustrating. The passage of time had obscured many aspects of the physical and social world described in the Old and New Testaments. To the people who had lived in those distant millennia and had walked across that land every day of their lives, the Bible would have been full of familiar details. However, those now pondering it sometimes found themselves entangled in a thicket of strange names, peculiar laws, and alien customs. Interest in the factual foundations of Scripture was strong, but anyone who visited the Holy Land and tried to learn where David had slain Goliath or where Jesus had performed a certain miracle was unlikely to get a reliable answer. Knowledge—uncertain even in the time of the empress Helena—had given way to vague surmise.

In the 19th century, that began to change. Legend and guesswork became increasingly unacceptable. The power of the mind to penetrate the unknown was being demonstrated in many areas, not the least of them the study of the past, and it seemed possible that the vistas of biblical history might be opened as well. Seeking answers in the soil of Palestine was certain to be a fiercely difficult job, especially since the exact location of many sites mentioned in the Bible had long been forgotten. Moreover, conditions in the countryside were primitive, the populace occasionally hostile, and the Islamic authorities wary of foreigners. But the desire to know outweighed all obstacles, and soon Palestine started to yield up its secrets. The pace was set by a brilliant American scholar named Edward Robinson—first in a long line of talented persons who, building on one another's work, would by the mid-20th century gain a remarkable understanding of the biblical world.

From earliest childhood, Robinson was intimately familiar with the Bible. Born in Connecticut in 1793, he was the son of a Congregationalist minister who had abandoned the pulpit for the plow, becoming a prosperous farmer. The son showed no such practical inclinations, devoting himself to academics and, as a college student, doing particularly well in Greek and mathematics. A few years later he attended the Andover Theological Seminary in Massachusetts, mastering ancient Hebrew in only two years. He continued his biblical studies in Europe, then began writing and teaching. In 1837, recognized as a scholar of rare gifts, he was offered the position of professor of biblical literature at the newly founded Union Theological Seminary in New York City. He accepted, on one condition—that before he took up his duties, he be allowed to visit Palestine, "the object of my ardent wishes," as he put it. The request was granted, and early in 1838 he arrived in Egypt, hoping, for a start, to trace the footsteps of Moses and the Israelites through Sinai to the Promised Land.

During the course of his travels over the next four months, Robinson was accompanied by a Protestant missionary named Eli Smith, a former student of his now based in Beirut. The two made a superb team. Smith spoke Arabic fluently and understood local customs. Robinson not only knew Hebrew and other ancient languages but also had read practically everything ever written about the Holy Land, including the journals of early pilgrims and explorers. He put little faith in the observations of these early investigators, despite their unshakable confidence in the accuracy of their reports. One fourth-century pilgrim, for example, declared that he had seen the tree where Abraham spoke with Yahweh and two angels, and had

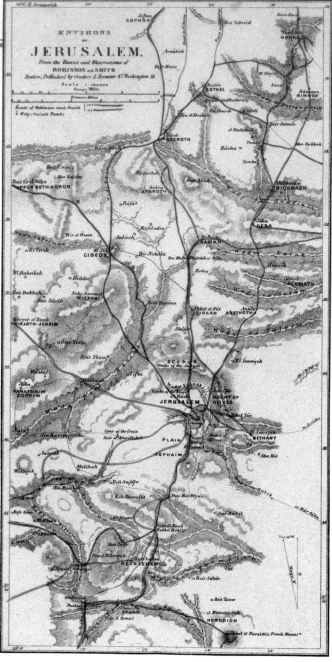

"The light of truth has gradually become dim," wrote Edward Robinson of his 1838 and 1852 excursions through Palestine in search of long-ago biblical sites— charted on this 19th-century map of Jerusalem's environs. Despite the shroud of millennia, the American scholar and his partner, Eli Smith, puzzled out some 100 ancient locations from their Arabic names—such as Anathoth (now Anata), birthplace of the prophet Jeremiah.

visited Job's farm. A later visitor told of recapturing a poignant moment not mentioned in the Bible: His guide had explained that a depression they had seen in a stone in Jerusalem was made by the hand of Jesus as he supported himself for a moment during the struggle toward Calvary under the burden of the cross. Such discoveries had been commonplace over the centuries—and were rarely questioned. Robinson saw in them "mistaken piety, credulous superstition, not unmingled with pious fraud." Early in his own trip, he confronted tradition head-on, dismissing the accepted site of Mount Sinai on the basis of his analysis of the description in Exodus.

But Robinson was convinced that at least some lost details of biblical geography could be recovered. Only a few decades earlier, surveyors in the employ of Napoleon Bonaparte, who had tried to extend French power into the Near East, had conducted a topographic study of portions of Palestine. They had made no attempt to link existing placenames with those in the Bible, but there was a way it could be done—and Robinson and Smith were exceptionally well qualified to do it.

The method involved a simple chain of linguistic logic. Hebrew was the language of the Old Testament, but it had eventually fallen into disuse and been supplanted by Aramaic, which Jesus spoke, and still later by Arabic. The Romans had attempted a sort of linguistic conquest when they replaced local geographical names with Latin versions. Among ordinary folk, however, this effort had been a failure: Because they found the new names difficult to pronounce, they usually stuck with the old ones. Nor had those old ones changed much with time, since Hebrew, Aramaic, and Arabic were all Semitic languages, related in many ways, including their sounds. Pondering this history, Robinson felt sure that the placenames of the Bible "have thus lived on upon the lips of the Arabs even unto our own day, almost in the same form in which they have also been transmitted to us in the Hebrew Scriptures."

He was right. As he and Smith trekked across the Palestinian landscape—taking compass bearings constantly and writing up detailed descriptions of the terrain each evening in their tent—they were able to establish numerous match-ups between modern and ancient names, a process much assisted by Robinson's encyclopedic knowledge of the Bible and related texts. A village called Beitin was

Bethel, where Jacob dreamed that God stood at the top of a ladder reaching to heaven and called down, "The land whereon thou liest, to thee will I give it, and to thy seed." Seilun had to be Shiloh, where Joshua founded a religious center to house the Ark of the Covenant, which held the Ten Commandments. In the same way, the two explorers identified Beth-shemesh (Ain-shems), where the Ark was returned to the Israelites after the Philistines captured it; the Vale of Elah, where David slew Goliath; and many additional sites—more than 100 in all. A phenomenal feat of historical retrieval, the findings amazed the world when they were published three years later. An admiring fellow scholar wrote, "It is not too much to say that Robinson's Biblical Researches are worth all the records of travel in the Holy Land from the time of the Savior down to the time when he published his work."

Robinson and Smith's investigations often called for an adventuresome spirit and no small measure of daring. In one notable instance, their scholarly curiosity led them quite literally into the tightest of spots. In the process, they did not just identify a location but actually discovered physical evidence—a remarkable piece of ancient engineering that had played a prominent part in an Old Testament story. The scene was Jerusalem.

Late in the eighth century BC, during the reign of Hezekiah, the city faced a possible siege by the Assyrian ruler Sennacherib. Hezekiah, drawing courage from the words of the prophet Isaiah, was determined to resist, which required ensuring the city's water supply. He ordered that an underground aqueduct be built from a spring known as Gihon, just east of Jerusalem, to the Pool of Siloam, within the city walls. His preparations proved wise: Sennacherib was repulsed when he attacked in 701 BC.

The tunnel is mentioned twice in the Bible, and Robinson also knew of it from several other references. One afternoon he and Smith went to the Pool of Siloam. By luck the water level was low, allowing access to the tunnel entrance. Taking off their shoes, the two men followed the passage. "At the end of 800 feet," Robinson later recalled, "it became so low that we could advance no further without crawling on all fours. As we were not prepared for this, we thought it better to retreat and try again another day from the other end." The entrance from the spring was blocked with loose stones. These were

First surveyed by Edward Robinson in 1838, Hezekiah's tunnel (above), *which connects Gihon spring* (inset, top) *with the Pool of Siloam* (opposite) *inside the walls of Jerusalem, brought vital stores of water to the city during the Assyrian siege of 701 BC. Even though the attacking leader Sennacherib boasted of shutting King Hezekiah in "like a bird in a cage," he neither flushed him out nor gained entrance to the city.*

removed, and Robinson and Smith crept along the serpentine course. "Most of the way we could indeed advance upon our hands and knees; yet in several places we could only get forward by lying at full length and dragging ourselves along on our elbows." Unperturbed, they finally reached the place where their earlier attempt had halted. The full length of the subterranean channel, they calculated, was 1,750 feet.

By studying chisel marks on the tunnel walls, Robinson deduced that the diggers had proceeded from both ends and met in the middle. Four decades later, a Jerusalem schoolboy's chance discovery not only confirmed his judgment but also added dramatic new details to the story. Venturing into the tunnel on a hot June day, the boy slipped in the water and, as he struggled to his feet, touched a smooth area on the rough rock wall. It seemed to bear some markings. When experts heard the boy's story, they soon came to investigate. Lowering the water level, they uncovered an inscription apparently carved to commemorate the completion of this remarkable project: ". . . And while there were still three cubits to be cut through, there was heard the voice of a man calling to his fellow, for there was an overlap in the rock on the right and on the left. And when the tunnel was driven through, the quarrymen hewed the rock, each man toward his fellow, ax against ax; and the water flowed from the spring toward the reservoir for 1,200 cubits, and the height of the rock above the heads of the quarrymen was 100 cubits." (A cubit was defined as the length of the forearm, or about 17 to 21 inches.)

As well as giving the moment immediacy nearly 3,000 years later, the inscription offered scholars a superb and long-sought example of early Hebrew writing. The words themselves had a wonderfully familiar ring. Said one exultant scholar, "The language of the inscription is the purest biblical Hebrew."

After investigating a number of sites in Jerusalem, Robinson and Smith concluded their whirlwind tour in the north, exploring the countryside of Galilee and the ancient realm of Samaria. Fueled in large part by their success, study of the Holy Land gathered momentum in the following decades. The leading vehicle for continued research was a British organization called the Palestine Exploration Fund (PEF), formed in 1865 for the express purpose of investigating

Accepting a book of Samaritan prayer, Lt. Charles Warren (near left) visits with the leader of the Samaritan community, Jakoob esh-Shellaby, in 1867, the year Warren discovered an underground system that probably supplied Jerusalem with water from ancient times through its Roman destruction in AD 70.

This cross-section diagram illustrates the remarkable system of tunnels and shafts that allowed the ancient inhabitants of Jerusalem to maintain their water supply from a source outside the city walls. The vertical shaft at left was possibly an aborted attempt by the original engineers to reach the underground channel below.

the "Archaeology, Geography, Geology, and Natural History of Palestine." Among its founders were a former prime minister and several other prominent statesmen—a sign that Britain had political as well as academic interests in the region. In fact, several European nations were keeping a close watch on the area: The Ottoman Empire was tottering, and new power arrangements seemed probable. Nonetheless, the fund was primarily a scholarly institution, seeking knowledge rather than influence. It was supported by public contributions, which came pouring in; Queen Victoria herself gave 150 pounds.

In 1867, the PEF assigned Lieutenant Charles Warren and other officers of the Royal Engineers to look for the biblical past in Jerusalem's very foundations. Warren was only 27 years old but already well seasoned in fieldwork, having built extensive fortifications on the Rock of Gibraltar during the previous seven years. Expert in all phases of military mining, he set about probing the area around the Temple Mount—the platform where the Jewish Temple had presumably once stood—by digging a series of shafts down to

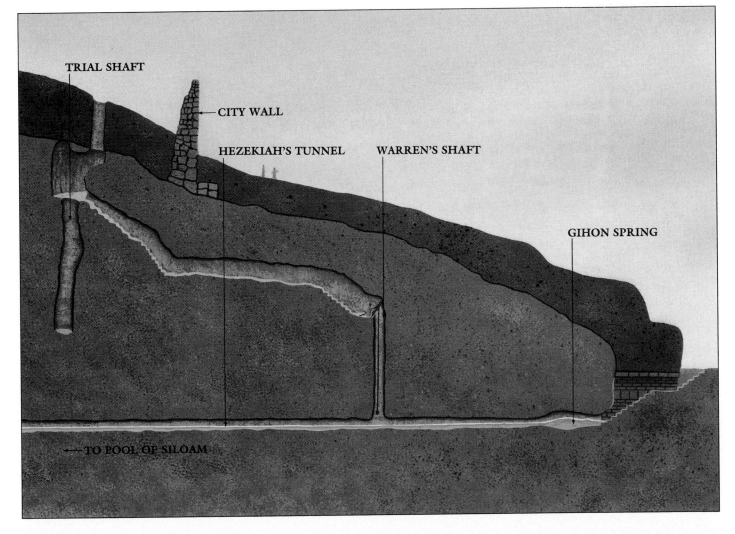

TRIAL SHAFT

CITY WALL

HEZEKIAH'S TUNNEL

WARREN'S SHAFT

GIHON SPRING

TO POOL OF SILOAM

bedrock and then tunneling laterally. This activity made the Ottoman authorities profoundly uneasy and spawned rumors that the British were planting bags of gunpowder with the intention of someday destroying the sacred Dome of the Rock and nearby mosques now occupying the mount. A natural diplomat as well as a daring engineer, Warren managed to keep the work going for months, doing much of the excavating at night.

As the engineers pushed through the subterranean debris, Warren traced part of the retaining walls of a temple and identified others of its structural features. (He had no way of dating these finds and believed they harked back to Solomon's Temple; in fact, they were remnants of construction ordered by King Herod in Roman times.) Warren also used his molelike skills to reconnoiter the city's ancient water-supply system. One channel, hidden for thousands of years, extended from the same spring that fed the aqueduct explored by Robinson and Smith. This one was far older, however—built in the 9th or 10th century BC. It led to a subterranean pool about 70 feet from the spring; buckets could be lowered to this pool through an 80-foot vertical shaft, which was itself reached by tunnels from the surface. The entire system would be named Warren's Shaft.

Warren turned out to be as dauntless in his exploring as Robinson. After finding the vertical shaft, he set about climbing it, accompanied by a Sergeant Birtles. Raising scaffolding as they went, they made their way up about 20 feet before stopping. As Warren recounted it: "On lighting a piece of magnesium wire at this point, we could see, 20 feet above us, a piece of loose masonry impending directly over our heads; and as several loose pieces had been found at the bottom, it occurred to both of us that our position was critical. Without speaking of it, we eyed each other ominously, and wished we were a little higher up." On they went, until one wall sloped off at a 45-degree angle, so that the shaft opened up into a huge cavern. The slope was covered with loose rock, but Warren fashioned a ladder and scrambled up. "The stones seemed all longing to be off; and one starting would have sent the mass rolling, and me with it, on top of the sergeant, all to form a mash at the bottom of the shaft." But the reconnaissance ended without incident, and after exploring some inner caverns the two returned safely to the bottom—unmashed.

British newspapers thrilled their readers with reports of Warren's excavations and tunnel-tracing exploits, and the publicity helped bring a freshet of contributions to the PEF. Warren himself left

DREAM COLLIDES WITH REALITY IN THE 19TH-CENTURY HOLY LAND

"The whole continent is leaning toward the East!" In 1829 French writer Victor Hugo voiced a growing passion—expressed in scholarship, art, and literature—that, before the century's close, would impel thousands to venture to the Holy Land. At first the exclusive retreat of the daring and the wealthy, the region attracted the middle classes too by the 1860s, with better access and affordable tour packages.

These pilgrims were drawn to the Holy Land not only by its rich biblical history (and, often, by a desire to clarify their faith) but also by a desire—implanted in them by colorful portrayals of camels in caravans, temptresses in harems, and dashing Bedouins on horseback—to experience the mystical and the exotic. To eager travelers from the West, the East promised to fulfill every dream from the spiritual to the profane.

English journalist Harriet Martineau sought religious quietude in her glimpse of Jerusalem; French novelist Gustave Flaubert traveled eastward for sexual adventure; and echoing the malaise of many Victorians, British explorer Sir Richard Burton wrote in 1878 of the opportunity "to

Circa 1865, British tourists rest beside Absalom's Tomb in Jerusalem. Built in the first century BC, the doubtfully named monument postdates King David's third son by nearly a thousand years.

Palestine and Syria

Programme of Arrangements for Visiting the Holy Land etc. etc.

Thos. Cook & Son
Chief Office
Ludgate Circus.
LONDON E.C.

An 1873 stereograph taken by American Benjamin Kilburn, one of many such images his firm sold door-to-door, shows the Western Wall, remnant of the enclosure around Herod's Temple.

Among the sightseers in this 1861 calotype of Jerusalem's Arch of Ecce Homo stands the Comte de Chambord, claimant to the French throne. The photographer, O. von Ostheim, probably hired himself out to tour groups.

escape the prison life of civilized Europe, and to refresh body and mind." From America, Herman Melville came to escape himself, despondent over *Moby Dick's* poor reception, and Mark Twain would sail into Beirut—an "innocent abroad"—spurred by curiosity and a love of travel.

Yet few were prepared for the reality that greeted them. "Palestine," wrote Twain, "sits in sackcloth and ashes," and Jerusalem itself exuded poverty, filth, and decay. "All around it stinks to die," Flaubert mourned. Flies and vermin crawled everywhere, though perhaps most bothersome was the ubiquitous flea: "How can a man think about Joshua or the valley of Jehoshaphat, when 50 indefatigable little bores are sharply reminding him of the actual and suffering

present?" complained American writer John William De Forest. He also summarized the sentiments aroused by innumerable shrines and keepsakes, commenting, "There is such an air of absurdity about most of the sacred localities and traditions that they excite unbelief and irreverence rather than faith and devotion."

Nonetheless, most took

home what they had come in search of, for the treasures of the East lived in the realm of the imagination. As Twain mused, "We think in bed, afterwards, when the glare and the noise and the confusion are gone, and in fancy we revisit alone the solemn monuments of the past and summon the phantom pageants of an age that has passed away."

Produced by Maison Bonfils, worldwide purveyors of Holy Land images, this view of the River Jordan with a camel and driver superimposed for effect typifies the studio's often staged—but popular—creations.

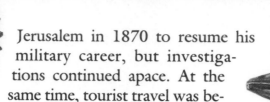

Jerusalem in 1870 to resume his military career, but investigations continued apace. At the same time, tourist travel was becoming increasingly popular. Regular steamship connections between European ports and Jaffa had existed for decades, a carriage road from Jaffa to Jerusalem had been built, and a massive surveying project, completed in 1880, provided excellent maps. In addition, the renowned travel authorities Karl Baedeker and Thomas Cook had published excellent guidebooks. They were careful not to mislead their readers: Easter in Jerusalem, said Baedeker, brings "many disorderly scenes which produce a painful impression," and he noted that the covered bazaars in the Old City "are very inferior to those of Cairo and Damascus and present no features of special interest." But the land of the Bible was an irresistible draw, and tourists arrived in ever greater numbers.

Archaeologists also continued to flock to the area, not just from Britain and America but also from Germany and France. Many brought with them a wider perspective. Whereas men like Robinson and Warren were primarily concerned with confirming the biblical record, the new generation of investigators tended to tackle more basic historical problems. Chief among these was how to date various finds so that they could be fitted into a coherent whole. The leader of this effort was a remarkable man named William Matthew Flinders Petrie. In 1890, in the space of just six weeks of digging, he revolutionized archaeology in the Holy Land, turning it into a science.

Petrie had become an archaeologist almost by instinct. He grew up in an intellectual household in Victorian England, but his formal schooling ceased after he suffered a collapse at the age of eight—the consequence of attempts by his mother, a talented linguist, to force-feed him Latin and Greek grammar. Thereafter, he read widely on his own, wandered the countryside studying old churches and Druid ruins, and became deeply interested in minerals, fossils, and ancient coins. At the age of 19, having remodeled an old theodolite and designed other surveying equipment with his father's help, he conducted an accurate survey of Stonehenge. Eight years later, he journeyed to Egypt, where his measurements of the Great Pyramid at Giza disproved a longstanding theory about the mystical significance of the structure's dimensions. The young man received praise and prize money from a British antiquarian society for his work, and he stayed in Egypt for the next 10 years, excavating a number of important sites and amassing a mountain of valuable information about Egyptian pottery. It was perhaps inevitable that his genius would be called upon to solve a problem in Palestine.

At that time, students of the Holy Land had begun to wonder about the nature of many small, rounded hills that dotted the landscape. These elevations were locally known as tells, from an Arabic word meaning "occupied mound." In the early 1870s, a German archaeologist named Heinrich Schliemann had caused a sensation by showing that a mound on the western coast of Asia Minor was not a natural feature but a layer cake of seven cities, each one built on the ruins of an earlier community—with the alleged Troy of Homer making up the seventh stratum. (Recent investigations have revealed a total of 10 layers, and scholars now believe Troy may have been the sixth.) It seemed quite possible that the mounds of Palestine, too, were the ruins of successive cities. Some of the tells even had names suggestive of biblical sites. The directors of the PEF were particularly interested in one hill several miles east of the town of Gaza. It was locally known as Khirbet Ajlan—perhaps an echo of Eglon, a Canaanite city that according to tradition had fallen to Joshua. They called Petrie in on the case.

Because he was interested in the historical relationship between Egypt and Palestine, Petrie agreed to help. A cursory examination, however, suggested to him that Khirbet Ajlan was no older than Roman times. Over the next few days, he cast about for a more promising site for Eglon, finally selecting a large mound called Tell el-Hesi, which rose 100 feet to a summit measuring 200 feet square. Its chief appeal was that it had already undergone a kind of natural excavation: A stream had eaten away one side of the tell, exposing its innards. The cut, said Petrie in his first report, "gives us at one stroke a series of all the varieties of pottery over a thousand years."

While working in Egypt, Petrie had realized that pottery was archaeological treasure. Previous excavators had simply thrown potsherds away, but he sensed that the humble stuff offered important clues to the ancient world. Earthen vessels were among the most commonplace domestic objects—serving as bowls, plates, jars, and so on. They broke easily and hence were replaced frequently, but unlike fabric or wood, they were almost impervious to decay or decomposition. Potsherds were thus abundant wherever people had lived.

Most important of all, pottery fashions changed over time,

Sir Flinders Petrie (below), *who first recognized the value of potsherds in archaeological dating, also discovered the finest jewelry ever to come from Canaan: Tell el-Ajjul, near Gaza, yielded a trove of ornaments roughly 3,500 years old, including a sheet-gold earring* (top, far left), *fly and larva amulets, and an embossed star pendant. A gold plaque of the goddess Asherah* (left) *shows a face whose "curiously impassive expression," in Petrie's estimation, might represent "the impartial rule of reproductive Nature."*

with each era favoring particular types of clay, specific methods of manufacture, and distinct stylistic features. Furthermore, these preferences tended to be shared throughout the Near East. Thus, if a layer representing an occupation level at an Egyptian site could be dated, corresponding layers elsewhere could be identified. Dating was neither easy nor foolproof; but inscriptions, seals, coins, and other sorts of historical indicators could serve to fix a layer and its pottery in time. In Egypt, Petrie had studied no fewer than three million pieces of pottery in the course of constructing a chronological framework that he considered reliable.

Building on this knowledge, he rapidly worked out a similar sequence for Tell el-Hesi, directing the labors of a large team of Arab diggers and personally examining about 50,000 potsherds. The excavation took him through 11 layers of occupation—a series of towns whose lineage stretched back hundreds of years before the time of Joshua. Petrie was confident that the links he had established between pottery types and particular periods were secure and would serve archaeologists throughout Palestine.

It was, in fact, an extraordinary achievement—not quite as chronologically correct as he believed, but a vast improvement on the guesswork that had prevailed until then. Initially, many scholars were reluctant to rely on pottery for dating, but later generations of investigators came to see the dig at Tell el-Hesi as a watershed event. As for the identity of the mound, Petrie speculated that it was Lachish, another Canaanite city conquered by Joshua, but he was apparently wrong: Modern research suggests that it was indeed Eglon. He had unwittingly achieved his original goal.

Palestine was by no means to Petrie's taste. He thought the laborers unreliable, the water almost undrinkable, and the sites less interesting than those in Egypt. To top it all off, on one occasion he was robbed and nearly choked to death by four assailants. It was thus without regret that, only four months after arriving, he returned to London and then went back to Egypt, where he continued to work for almost four decades more. But his contributions to the understanding of the Holy Land were not finished. While excavating the mortuary temple of the pharaoh Merenptah in the ancient city of Thebes in 1896, he discovered a black granite slab bearing 28 lines of inscription. The monumental stone, or stele, listed victories over

JUST WHO WAS THE PHARAOH OF EXODUS?

By the time Ramses II succumbed to old age, after a reign of nearly 70 years, he had outlived a full dozen of his sons. Thus the 13th in line, Merenptah, was already 60 when he ascended to a decade of power, around 1212 BC. Merenptah was believed by many to be the pharaoh of the Exodus, who pursued Moses and the Hebrews to the banks of the Red Sea. Although the Bible does not explicitly say so, it had been assumed that he perished with his army, engulfed by waters that had miraculously parted for the children of Israel. But when the mummy of Ramses' successor *(inset opposite)* actually turned up in 1898, it caused consternation among some

members of the clergy. Churchmen visiting Cairo were relieved when the archaeologist who had examined the body told them that it bore traces of salt, which they believed offered proof of the pharaoh's death in the Red Sea. He neglected to tell them that such deposits appear on most mummies—for the simple reason that embalmers used natron salts to dehydrate the flesh.

But it is Sir Flinders Petrie's so-called Israel stele *(left)*, discovered in Thebes in 1896, that seems to rule out Merenptah as the pharaoh of Exodus. The 10-foot-high stone, which lists his military conquests, predates the next-earliest reference to Israel by 400 years. Here, Merenptah boasts of subduing the Israelites as a people who were clearly settled in a home territory. Since he reigned for only 10 years, he could not have both vanquished them and been in power during their flight from Egypt, for, by the Bible's reckoning, the Jews wandered at least 40 years in the wilderness before reaching the Promised Land. It is far more likely, then, that Moses departed under the rule of Merenptah's father, Ramses II, whose name actually appears in the Book of Exodus appended to that of a city that was built, according to the Bible, by Hebrew slaves.

various enemies during Merenptah's reign, which, according to the thinking of some scholars, began in 1212 BC. One line read, "Israel is destroyed, its seed is not." This was—and still is—the oldest mention of the Israelites ever discovered. At dinner on the day he worked out the inscription, Petrie said to a companion, "This stele will be better known in the world than anything else I have found."

The tells of the Holy Land continued to be intensively scrutinized. In 1892 Frederick Bliss, an American archaeologist who had been chosen to carry on Petrie's work at Tell el-Hesi, came upon a tablet that helped refine his predecessor's dating scheme. Discovered under a layer of ash that marked a destruction of the city, the tablet was inscribed in a version of cuneiform identical to that found at the site of Tell el-Amarna in Egypt and securely dated to the 14th century BC. Not only did this anchor the stratum in time, but it also gave proof of Egyptian control of Canaanite city-states during the period.

As the 19th century drew to a close, the PEF appointed a young Irish archaeologist named Robert Alexander Stewart Macalister to assist Bliss in the investigation of other tells and establish their links to the Bible. Although they worked together for a few years, their personalities clashed, and Bliss soon retired. Macalister went on alone to direct the excavation of a mound identified as the city of Gezer, mentioned in Egyptian and Mesopotamian records as well as in the Bible. There he turned up the earliest known Hebrew inscription—a list of agricultural activities written in verse form, probably for easy memorization by children, and composed in the 10th century BC, the time of Solomon.

With the passing years, the examination of tells in the Holy Land became more and more systematic, but the Bible remained the driving force behind most of the searches. In 1908, backed by funds from the New York banker and philanthropist Jacob Schiff, the American archaeologist George Reisner and his assistant Clarence Fisher began probing a mound thought to be the site of an important city mentioned in the First Book of Kings. Here, supposedly, was Samaria, capital of the northern kingdom of Israel. It had been founded in the ninth century BC by King Omri, who, according to Scripture, had purchased the land from a man named Shemer "for two talents of silver." Like Petrie, Reisner had worked extensively in

Egypt and would do so again, achieving fame particularly for his efforts at Giza. He brought with him to Palestine a skilled force of surveyors, draftsmen, photographers, and Egyptian foremen. Local Arabs did the heavy lifting, and they were driven hard. A stickler for discipline, Reisner issued a list of regulations requiring the laborers to come to work every day, obey orders without fail, always fill their baskets to the brim, and never fight or quarrel. "But ordinary work songs were encouraged," said Reisner, "as they helped to pass away the tedium of the day."

Proceeding methodically down through the mound, the team kept track of the location and nature of every scrap of material they came upon. Their finds included many inscribed fragments of pottery that bore personal names and described an ancient trade in wine and oil. This documentation of daily life was certainly fascinating, but the most dramatic discovery had biblical connections: a layer of ash recording Samaria's doom. The city was destroyed when the Assyrians overran the area in 722 BC—a disaster that befell the Israelites, according to the Second Book of Kings, because "they obeyed not the voice of the Lord their God, but transgressed his covenant, and all that Moses the servant of the Lord commanded, and would not hear them, nor do them."

Modern Palestine was about to undergo convulsions of its own. The Ottoman Empire was on its last legs, and World War I would bring it to ruin. Allying themselves with Germany, the Ottomans soon found the conflict on their doorstep; in 1916, British forces invaded the Holy Land, gradually grinding down the opposition and capturing Jerusalem in late 1917. Britain's foreign secretary, Lord Balfour, then set in motion a more protracted struggle for the land by issuing a declaration supporting the establishment of "a national home for the Jewish people"—the dream of the Zionist movement, launched two decades earlier. All along, the British intended to maintain firm control in the region, but the passions unleashed by the Balfour Declaration were too old and too fierce to be checked. As early as 1918, Jews and Arabs were at each other's throats. Thirty years later, Britain would withdraw from the scene.

Despite the unrest, archaeological studies went on, more energetically than ever. Some of the postwar projects were of marathon duration. From 1925 to 1939, for example, excavators labored in

A pair of gold-foil figurines from the early 15th century BC, found at Gezer, show the influence of Syria in their tall headgear and collar necklaces (above). *Northward in Samaria, where Ahab is said in Kings to have built an ivory palace, these carved lions—less than two inches high— were found among 500 fragments of the substance considered as precious as gold.*

The head of an anthropoid clay sarcophagus unearthed at the site of Beth-shan displays a feather headdress typical of Philistine apparel. After the Israelite king Saul fell upon his sword, the Philistines hung his body from Beth-shan's walls.

northern Palestine at a place called Megiddo, site of the strategic biblical city of Armageddon. (It had been fought over so often that the New Testament Revelation of John appropriated its name in prophesying a war that would end the world.) The diggers at Megiddo penetrated through 20 occupation layers stretching back to the fifth millennium BC. Over a 12-year span beginning in 1921, archaeologists probed just as deeply into the past at the site of the biblical city of Beth-shan. Here, as recounted in the First Book of Samuel, the first Israelite monarch, Saul, fell on his sword after his sons were killed in a battle against the Philistines. David avenged him by conquering the city.

Some of the most productive work was accomplished under the auspices of the American Schools of Oriental Research (ASOR), an institute formed in 1900 by more than 20 universities, colleges, and theological schools. In 1920, ASOR gained a new director in Jerusalem, 29-year-old William Foxwell Albright, already a leading scholar in studies of the ancient Near East. Born in Chile to Methodist missionary parents, Albright had grown up in dreadful circumstances and was extremely nearsighted; but he was cast in the mold of such great forerunners as Edward Robinson and Flinders Petrie, possessing a towering intellect and an equally formidable gift for detail. He could read many ancient languages, had acquired prodigious historical knowledge, knew the Bible through and through, and delighted in the intricacies and minutiae of scientific excavation.

Spending much of his time as a hands-on archaeologist at various digs throughout the region, Albright greatly advanced Petrie's pottery-based dating method, working out a much more detailed classification scheme and solidifying the chronology. He gave up his post as director of the Jerusalem School of ASOR in 1936, but for three decades more he continued to exert enormous influence as a teacher and writer. Like almost all of those who had preceded him, he never lost sight of the biblical dimension in his researches. And he felt confident that archaeology had served the Scriptures well. The Bible, he wrote, "no longer appears as an absolutely isolated monument of the past, as a phenomenon without relation to its environment. It now takes its place in a context which is becoming better known every year." Even more to the good, as far as Albright was concerned, "nothing tending to disturb the religious faith of Jew or Christian has been discovered."

From Lachish, during the Babylonian destruction of the kingdom of Judah in 587 BC, a military officer writes to his commander: "May Yahweh cause my lord to hear news of peace, even now, even now" (inset). After the first letters written on potsherds were discovered in 1934, children were sent to sift through the dirt at Lachish for other fragments.

The historicity of the biblical narrative received another boost in the 1930s when the British archaeologist John Starkey corrected Petrie's error made four decades earlier and found the true site of Lachish, the scene of many biblical struggles beginning in the days of Joshua. Even more dramatically than at Samaria, a layer of ash yielded eloquent testimony to the city's fate. Among the ashes Starkey found 21 pottery fragments bearing Hebrew inscriptions that turned out to be letters written to a Judean officer by a subordinate as Babylonian warriors led by the emperor Nebuchadnezzar stormed across the land in 588 BC. The letters mostly dealt with military matters, but the words resonated with a sense of dread that the southern kingdom of Judah was about to fall. "And let (my lord) know," the soldier wrote, "that we are watching over the beacon of Lachish, according to the signals which my lord hath given, for Azekah is not to be seen." The city of Azekah had just been destroyed by Nebuchadnezzar, who next razed Lachish, then besieged Jerusalem. That city fell in the summer of 586 BC, and Nebuchadnezzar brutally punished its resistance. The king of Judah was blinded, his sons were executed, the Temple constructed by Solomon was demolished, and much of the population was sent into exile in Babylonia.

More discoveries lay ahead, although not for Starkey, who was murdered by Arab bandits in 1938. In the years after the establishment of the modern state of Israel in 1948, a Jewish perspective finally rose to prominence, after having been given short shrift at best during the years of Arab and then British rule. For Israeli archaeologists, as well as for those from other nations, the Bible remained a potent resource. In fact, archaeologists have estimated that the Holy Land contains about 6,000 sites that relate in some way to the people and places and events of Scripture. Even so, many modern scholars—applying what is known as the New Archaeology—have become more interested in finding out what they can about ancient Holy Land cultures with little or no reference to the Bible, relying as much as possible solely on the tales told by artifacts. But the age-old stories of faith still hold their place for many in the field. In the words of the eminent American archaeologist William Dever, a century and a half of exploration "has for all time demolished the notion that the Bible is pure mythology. The Bible is about real, flesh-and-blood people, in a particular time and place, whose actual historical experience led them irrevocably to a vision of the human condition and promise that transcended anything yet conceived in antiquity."

A PAINTER'S PILGRIMAGE

Seeking spiritual fulfillment, historical enlightenment, and even holy vengeance, for centuries untold millions have ventured to the heavenly crescent bordering the Mediterranean to walk the lands of the Bible. But when, in August 1838, the Scotsman David Roberts embarked on his sojourn into the dramatic regional backdrop of so much of the Old and New Testaments, he was fueled solely by a passion for artistic opportunity. Having already toured the cities of Europe to draw their breathtaking edifices, the rising 42-year-old painter would find this journey to be the most rewarding of his career.

Roberts headed northward in February 1839 from Egypt, where he had committed the mighty monuments of the pharaohs to his sketchbook. Despite a panoply of discomforts, his enthusiasm of purpose never waned as he generated drawing after drawing—some 300 in all—including biblical landmarks from Sinai to Canaan to Upper Galilee. In conveying the beauty and glory of the landscapes, he often romanticized or idealized them; however, Roberts did render architectural structures with an honesty that is praised by scholars today. His illustration of Mount Sinai *(right)*—where Exodus tells of Moses receiving the Ten Commandments—embellishes the soaring height of the peak while faithfully detailing the Convent of Saint Catherine, a sixth-century AD monastery housing 3,000 biblical manuscripts.

After his return to London in July of the same year, Roberts converted the delicate sketches into watercolors and negotiated their publication. Between 1842 and 1849, the works, reproduced as lithographs, were published in five volumes titled *The Holy Land*, which featured the above drawing of the artist, alongside a dedication to Queen Victoria. A sampling of the images—which earned Roberts world reknown—appears on the following pages, a small visual pilgrimage tracing the artist's route through antiquity.

Named in the Old Testament as one of Canaan's earliest cities, and later to become the greatest of the Five Cities of the Philistines, Gaza crowns a hill near the Mediterranean coast, its 1839 skyline punctuated by mosques. Here, betrayed by Delilah, Samson, in a last display of might, pulled the Temple of Dagon down onto his captors' heads, crying, "Let me die with the Philistines."

a Saba. April 1839.

"*The heights are wild,*" *wrote Roberts of the wilderness of En Gedi, on the western shore of the Dead Sea. David sought refuge from the persecution of Saul among the steep hills and ravines, which here harbor a monastery named after Saint Saba, a fifth-century Christian monk.*

Prominent in the holy city of Jerusalem is the seventh-century AD Mosque of Omar, or Dome of the Rock (background, right), *built atop the remnants of Solomon's and Herod's temples. It marks the place on Mount Moriah where Abraham brought his son Isaac to sacrifice to God, as well as the spot where, Muslims believe, Muhammad ascended to heaven. In the foreground, pilgrims are shown praying in the direction of the Church of the Holy Sepulcher, thought to be the burial site of Jesus.*

Behind Arabs on horseback, the ruins of ancient Samaria, renamed Sebaste by Herod in the first century BC, spread across a basin in the fertile country 40 miles north of Jerusalem. Founded around 900 BC by Omri, the father of Ahab, Samaria was the capital of the northern kingdom of Israel until 722 BC. Most of the remains are vestiges of the many monuments Herod built throughout the land that he dedicated to the emperor Augustus Caesar.

CITIES OF THE PROMISED LAND

Two startlingly well preserved relics of the Canaanite city-state of Hazor, a 3,200-year-old clay mask and above it the two halves of a potter's wheel rest exactly as found by archaeologists in the 1950s.

Under a remorseless sun, the Israeli excavators steadily cut their trench deeper into the earthen rampart guarding the western flank of the ancient city of Hazor, about 10 miles north of the Sea of Galilee. They had been at work for a number of days and so far had found nothing in this section of the huge site but beaten earth and fieldstones. Then, digging down farther, they came upon something altogether different: a tiny statue—scarcely more than 15 inches tall—of a seated, headless man. The leader of the excavation, Yigael Yadin, immediately directed that the trench be enlarged in the area around the statue. Proceeding with barely contained excitement, the team members soon uncovered a small basalt slab that had apparently served as an altar, and behind it a set of upright pillars, all made to the same reduced scale; and just a little deeper, near the base of the statue, lay the detached head, which had clearly been broken off by a single sharp blow.

It was obvious right away that what they had found was some sort of miniature temple, believed to be a shrine to the Canaanite god Baal Hamman. Looking at the decapitated statue, Yadin was sure that the sanctuary had been deliberately defiled. And he had few doubts as to the perpetrators. Deeply familiar with his own Hebrew Bible, he recalled the exhortation to faithful Jews in the 12th chapter of Deuteronomy: "Ye shall utterly destroy all the places, wherein the nations which ye shall possess served their gods, upon the high mountains, and upon the hills, and under every green tree: And ye shall overthrow their altars, and break their pillars, and burn their groves with fire; and ye shall hew down the graven images of their gods, and destroy the names of them out of that place."

Yadin had begun excavating the ruined city only a few months before, in August of 1955, a hard time for his recently reborn nation. The site was relatively close to Israel's Lebanese border—not exactly the securest area of the beleaguered Jewish state. From the nearby Golan Heights, Syrian artillery regularly sought targets among the collective farming communities, or kibbutzes, in the area, and settlers stood armed guard at night against infiltrators from the north.

More than 3,000 years earlier, Hazor had known similar alerts, but in that epoch the threat had apparently come from the south, as the Israelites advanced to lay claim to their Promised Land. Even then the city was ancient: Egyptian texts and Mesopotamian archives dating from before the 18th century BC make mention of its kings. But the literary references that most interested Yadin came from the Bible. The Book of Joshua opens just after the death of Moses, when the Lord commands Joshua to "go over this Jordan, thou, and all this people, unto the land which I do give to them, even

Furnishings of a small religious sanctuary at Hazor include these nine upright stone steles as well as a deftly carved lion, a rough basalt offertory slab, and a seated figure of a deity whose head had been neatly lopped off, perhaps by conquering Israelites about 1250 BC. On the center stele a pair of carved hands rise in supplication toward the crescent-and-disk symbol of what may be the Canaanite moon god or Asherah, the mother goddess.

to the children of Israel." The text goes on to detail a string of triumphs over Canaanite strongholds, culminating with the victory over Hazor: "And Joshua at that time turned back, and took Hazor, and smote the king thereof with the sword: for Hazor beforetime was the head of all those kingdoms. And they smote all the souls that were therein with the edge of the sword, utterly destroying them: there was not any left to breathe: and he burnt Hazor with fire."

Yadin himself was well qualified to reconstruct such an onslaught, assuming that it had indeed occurred. Like Joshua in the 13th century BC, he had been a soldier of Israel, and a high-ranking one at that. The son of a distinguished archaeologist and trained in the same discipline, Yadin had set aside his academic interests in the 1930s to join the Jewish underground military force in Palestine known as Haganah, rising to become its chief of operations and later chief of staff of the fledgling Israeli army during the war of independence in 1948. Archaeology might seem a useless apprenticeship for a general, but his knowledge of forgotten Roman roads turned out to be a great advantage to an army seeking secure supply routes in the face of numerically superior enemies. On one occasion, in a surprise night attack against an Egyptian unit, he ordered his troops along an ancient roadway that had been lost beneath sand dunes for almost 2,000 years; the Israeli soldiers appeared from an entirely unexpected direction, and the startled Egyptian commander was captured still wearing his pajamas.

Later in life, Yadin would serve as Israel's deputy prime minister under Menachem Begin; but a few years after the war, he was ready to apply his formidable organizational skills to his original calling. He chose Hazor as the subject of his country's first major excavation partly because little was then known of either Canaanite or Israelite settlements in Galilee, and partly because of the many references to the city in ancient sources. He recognized that the site might offer a particularly promising opportunity to compare documentary evidence with what the spade could uncover. And he would bring to the research a new and entirely Israeli attitude. Like William Albright and earlier biblical archaeologists who had sought to verify the great stories of faith by digging, Yadin and his colleagues took the Bible very seriously indeed. But for the Israelis, there was a secular as well as a sacred dimension to the Scriptures. Even among those who did not count themselves believers, the Bible was an essential and irre-

51

placeable document, the repository of their national history and the foundation of their national pride.

By the 20th century, all that was left of biblical Hazor was a tell, a bottle-shaped mound of about 25 acres. Below the tell stretched an enclosure eight times as large, surrounded by earthen ramparts and a moat. A brief, probing dig in the 1920s had identified the mound as Hazor. The enormous and apparently empty enclosure, however, was another matter, and it had been puzzling Yadin ever since he first reconnoitered the site during military maneuvers in the late 1940s. Most scholars believed that the vast rectangle was some kind of fortified encampment; early investigators had even jokingly suggested that it was a parking lot for chariots. But the colossal labor that must have been involved to raise the massive earthworks seemed to belie both serious and idle speculation. Although his main effort was devoted to the Hazor tell, when Yadin began his excavation in the summer of 1955 he assigned a backup team to begin trenching the 200-acre "camp."

Initial results there were disappointing: The whole area had been under the plow for centuries, and the earth seemed to have no secrets left to reveal. But as the spades and trowels of Yadin's volunteers probed deeper, they soon encountered the walls and floors of an extensive cluster of dwellings. In addition to the tell above, the great enclosure now also appeared to have been a city. In fact, it had been several cities, each built upon the ruins of its predecessor.

The discovery proved that Hazor had been much larger than previously imagined. Using a then-standard formula for calculating the number of inhabitants in a given area, Yadin figured that the population had perhaps been as high as 40,000. (A more recent formula, based on an average of 100 inhabitants per acre, suggests a still-impressive total of about 20,000.) Potsherds indicated that the latest occupation of what the team was now calling the lower city had been near the middle of the 13th century BC, and other evidence showed that the end had not been peaceful. Heat-cracked stones, scorch marks, and a layer of ashes made it plain that the city had died by fire, while floors scattered with intact pottery testified that the inhabitants had left in a hurry, if they had survived at all.

For Yadin, there could be no doubt as to the agency of destruction. The 11th chapter of Joshua told the story: "But as for the cities that stood still in their strength, Israel burned none of them,

Israeli soldier and archaeologist Yigael Yadin prepares to photograph part of his large pioneering dig at Hazor. In five years of excavations, Yadin uncovered no fewer than 20 layers of buildings, indicating that the city dated back to the Chalcolithic period and was built and rebuilt over a period of 3,000 years.

Hazor's ruined walls crown a rocky, steep-sided knob that looks down on a fertile, well-watered valley. Strongly fortified, rich with foodstuffs, and strategically located on the main north-south caravan route between Damascus and the south, Hazor was the most important city in the northern hills of Galilee during the heyday of Canaanite power.

save Hazor only; that did Joshua burn." Confirmation seemed to follow when Yadin's main excavation force reached a comparable occupation layer in the tell itself—the upper city. Once more, there were unmistakable signs of fire and total destruction, sometime between 1250 and 1230 BC.

Unlike the lower city, however, the upper city had been rebuilt, and because of the upside-down, time-reversed nature of archaeology, the excavators already knew something about these later years. For a century or more after the devastation, the city's ruins were home to a seminomadic group—probably the early Israelites themselves—who constructed little or nothing of consequence. About 950 BC, a fortified settlement was erected on part of the ancient tell, with walls and gates fashioned by King Solomon's masons; by the time of King Ahab, in the ninth century BC, buildings covered the old upper city. In subsequent decades these too were destroyed, first by an earthquake and then by the invading Assyrians in 732 BC. Thereafter, although archaeologists found scattered remains, Hazor was never again revived as a full-fledged city.

Yadin's work had advanced the cause of those such as Albright, who tended to believe in the biblical version of the Israelites' arrival in Canaan. For the Exodus from Egypt, there was not likely ever to be archaeological verification: Wandering nomads do not usually leave traces of themselves that endure for 3,000 years. But after his discoveries at Hazor, Yadin was convinced that the conquest itself had taken place essentially as narrated in the Book of Joshua.

However, there was other, opposing, evidence, and it came from the Bible itself. No one disagreed that toward the end of the 13th century BC, the Israelites had established themselves as a significant presence in Canaan. It was a time of transition, from the era known to archaeologists as the late Bronze Age to the early Iron Age (when increasing numbers of peoples were learning to smelt iron ore and turn it into much sturdier weapons and implements). The Merenptah stele *(pages 32-33),* which specifically mentions a people called Israel, was dated to the same period. But the stele explained neither who the Israelites were nor how they had come to prominence. For that information, the Bible remained the prime source—a source that was ambiguous, if not downright contradictory.

From the Book of Exodus up to the end of Joshua, the ac-

NEW METHODS FOR OLD SITES:
A REVOLUTION IN THE FIELD

Archaeologists once had to rely on tape measures and other fairly simple devices to survey a site and choose the most promising spot to excavate. But today—in the Holy Land, as elsewhere in the world—they have access to an astonishing array of technologies, including lasers, advanced computer-imaging systems, and atomic energy. The precision of their new tools has created a time-and-resource-saving revolution.

This became evident in a survey at Caesarea Maritima, the Mediterranean port city built by King Herod. Here archaeologists employed a theodolite, a traditional surveying instrument that gauges elevations and angles. But this was a theodolite with a difference: It had an infrared laser, as well as a calculator that determined the angle and distance traveled by the beam. Thus equipped, it

was able to take into account the curvature of the earth, barometric pressure, and temperature, and it was accurate to within $1/1,000$ of a foot.

The archaeologists were intrigued by surviving sections of a sixth-century AD fortress wall. They calculated that if they could trace its former course around a certain theater, they could tell how large an area it had enclosed. Taking only a

couple of hours for what normally would have required days, the laser theodolite revealed that two portions of the walls, previously thought to be out of alignment on the basis of an inaccurate earlier survey done with an old-fashioned theodolite, in fact lined up and belonged together. This helped the excavators to understand and project the shape and design of the fortress itself.

A map generated by computer shows sections of a fortress wall around a theater (purple) *surveyed inaccurately in the past* (yellow, right), *with the position corrected* (red dots) *by laser theodolite* (inset).

MAKING THE INVISIBLE VISIBLE

Countless hours have been spent by archaeologists pondering the best spot to dig, and many more have been wasted in fruitless excavation. To increase accuracy, two wonders of modern technology are now being employed: One relies on electromagnetism to reveal underground features, and the other offers a view of what a site probably looked like in past eras.

Put to work in the Holy Land, the first of these devices helped find Ammonite fortifications that may have been breached by none other than King David. The site, Tell el-Umeiri, on the northern fringe of Jordan's Madaba Plains, was assumed to be Abel-Keramim, an Ammonite city mentioned in the Bible. Seeking its most promising subsurface locale, archaeologists turned to GPR, or ground-penetrating radar. As it is pulled across the ground, this sledlike device sends continuous electromagnetic impulses into the earth. Bouncing back from obstructions, these impulses reveal the presence of walls of tombs and tunnels, among other things. The GPR at Tell el-Umeiri located defense walls destroyed about 1000 BC, the time of David's military campaigns.

Meanwhile, at another Jordanian locale, Wadi Hasa, archaeologists were searching for ancient settlements. They entered the details of their finds and also the results of an earlier survey into a computer using Geographic Information Systems (GIS), the first software able to map spatial data in three dimensions. When fed information about water sources, land contours, soils, animals, and vegetation, GIS can provide a picture of life in various geologic, prehistoric, and historical periods. The computer achieves this by translating the data into a series of environmental images that progress through the millennia showing ecological changes—from forest, say, to grassland and then desert. Since human beings choose habitats on the basis of natural resources, the archaeologists were able to use these glimpses of Wadi Hasa's past to predict where early settlements were most likely to have sprung up, such as at sites that had more water than others. Thus they could begin their digging with a high probability of success.

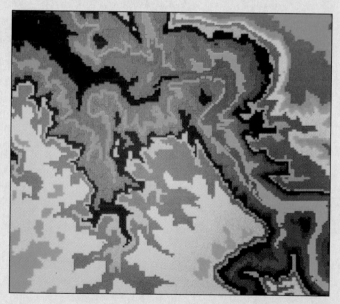
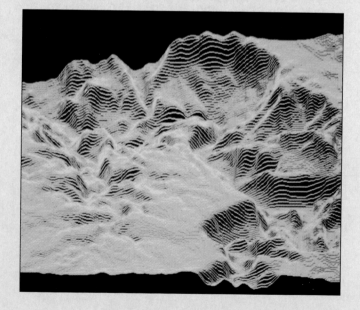

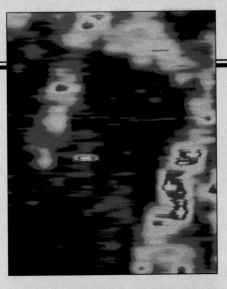

A scientist pulls a ground-penetrating radar (GPR) unit across the earth at Tell el-Umeiri in Jordan (inset). Meanwhile, a computer stationed nearby continuously receives, enhances, and displays the instrument's signals, shown in a printout segment (left), in which gray signifies the presence of buried stone. After absorbing this data, the computer generates an image like the one at right, showing buried walls in patterns of red, yellow, and light blue.

Geographic Information Systems produced the maps opposite, which show a region of Jordan's Wadi Hasa reconstructed from land contour data—slope, elevation, and distance. The image on the far left expresses elevation through color: Black represents the lowest areas, dark green the highest. A dry riverbed snakes from upper left to lower right. The same area is seen in the adjacent image (left); this time the computer has generated a three-dimensional contour map.

A photo of the excavation at Tell el-Umeiri (above) shows the section of a double casemate wall (area adjacent to inset) found on the western slope at the location confirmed by GPR. Below it is a steep earthwork rampart, and, at the bottom, a moat. This defense system was demolished about 1000 BC, when the Ammonites controlled the city. The battle between King David and the Ammonites recorded in 2 Sam. 10-12 may have been the very event in which this fortification was destroyed.

FINGERPRINTING CLAY AND POTS

Like people, artifacts often start out in one place and end up in another. Archaeologists, seeking insights into trade and migration, have long wanted to be able to identify the sources of pots originating at sites other than where they were found. Now—with the help of a nuclear reactor—precise knowledge of these origins is available.

A process called neutron activation analysis (NAA) enables scientists to examine the telltale composition of clay. All clays are made up of dozens of elements, and with NAA, the concentration of 20 to 30 of these elements can be measured. Earth from different locations varies slightly in the proportions of the elements it contains, and these minute differences provide clay from any given area with an identification akin to a fingerprint.

The process begins with the pulverization of a tiny chip from a piece of pottery. The powder is then irradiated by neutrons in a nuclear reactor, causing the elements present to emit gamma rays. These emissions enable the scientists to figure out the composition of the pottery.

They then compare its makeup to that of pottery taken from other locales.

The method proved its worth at Tel Dan, in northern Israel, where late Bronze Age remains of the biblical tribe of Dan have been studied. Among these were storage jars, less than a third of which NAA showed to have been produced at the site. The oldest jars were in fact made from clay at the tell, by the Danites themselves. But they were the narrow-mouthed, collared-rim type associated with southern Israel. This finding supports the biblical contention that the Danites moved from the south to the north.

The remaining pottery came from several different locales. Using NAA , the archaeologists could pinpoint locations for some of these, such as a large rounded vase adorned with chariots that they believed was the work of a particular Greek painter whose pieces had turned up in Israel, Turkey, and Greece. By comparing its composition with pottery samples found near both Mycenae and Tiryns, in Greece, they were indeed able to say that the vase originated at Mycenae.

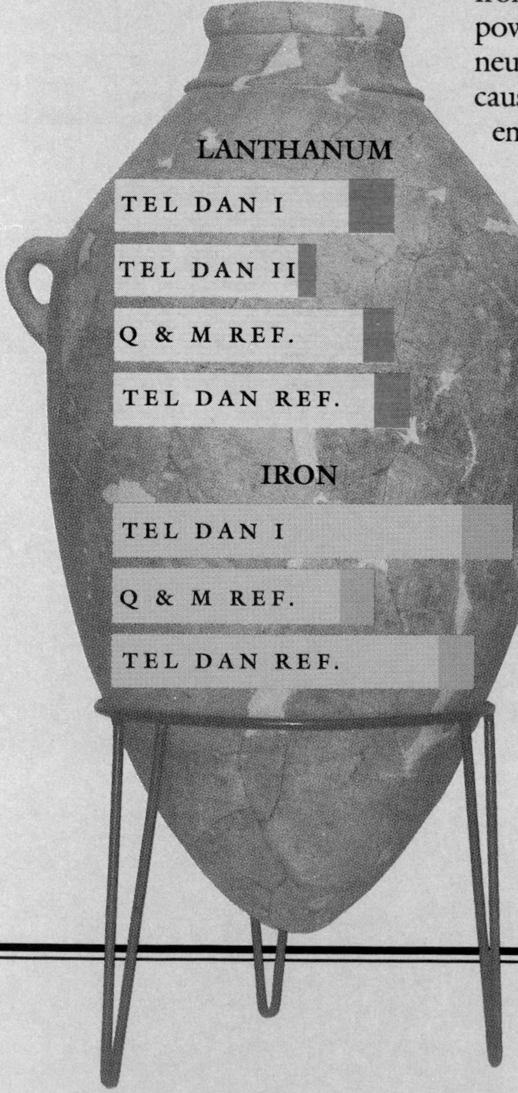

LANTHANUM

TEL DAN I

TEL DAN II

Q & M REF.

TEL DAN REF.

IRON

TEL DAN I

Q & M REF.

TEL DAN REF.

This restored collared-rim jar (left) was among the pieces from Tel Dan that underwent neutron activation analysis to determine its origin. Two groups of jars, labeled Tel Dan I and II, were compared with two reference groups—one known to have been made at Tel Dan, the other at sites known as Q and M. The graph shows that based on the presence of the element lanthanum, the Tel Dan II samples could not have originated at Tel Dan or at Q or M, but that the Tel Dan I jars could have come from either site. (The darker shadings show the standard deviations.) In iron content, the Tel Dan I jars matched only the Tel Dan group. Matches were confirmed for more than 18 other elements as well.

count is clear enough. After a lengthy journey during which Moses must constantly remind his people of their obligations to Yahweh, their god, the Israelites arrive at the borders of Canaan. There, under Moses' successor, Joshua, they prepare for holy war, then seize the country in three whirlwind campaigns. The last part of Joshua relates the division of the conquered territories among the 12 tribes of Israel.

The subsequent Book of Judges tells the story very differently. The destruction wrought by Joshua seems never to have occurred. Instead, there are long lists of Canaanite cities that were not captured at all, and even Hazor escapes for a time. The fourth chapter of Judges tells how its king had "nine hundred chariots of iron; and twenty years he mightily oppressed the children of Israel." Hazor's forces are destroyed only when the Hebrew prophetess Deborah takes charge, during a battle far from the city in the Valley of Esdraelon; afterward, the city's greatest general is murdered by treachery. Throughout most of the rest of the book the theme is one of recurring crisis, as time after time the Canaanites come close to annihilating the Israelites. In essence, Judges replaces Joshua's rapid conquest with a lengthy period—apparently from the 12th to the 10th century—during which the Israelites frequently live at peace with their neighbors, often intermarrying and sharing their culture to such an extent that their leaders are continually haranguing them on the evils of adopting false gods. The judges themselves are charismatic elders, not warriors, who take on the role of military commanders only when necessary, sometimes successfully, sometimes not.

There is no real way to reconcile the two narratives, although biblical scholars have gone some distance toward explaining their differences. Most modern authorities agree that the present texts of the first seven books of the Bible—comprising the five books of Moses known as the Pentateuch, plus Joshua and Judges—were compiled during the seventh century BC from various sources at least 200 years older. The prime purpose of their editors was not so much to write an accurate history in the modern sense as to create an account of the relationship between Yahweh and his chosen people. The Judges material, which comes from among the oldest sources, seems to have been deliberately subordinated to the far more ideologic Joshua text. In other words, the Judges story may have been closer to what actually happened, but the Joshua version represented the theological message that later generations of priests and elders hoped to impress upon the people. The Book of Joshua put the

Lush modern farms nestle behind the sunbaked rise that was the ancient city of Jericho, scarred by trenches left by a series of archaeological digs. In the earthquake-prone Great Rift Valley just north of the Dead Sea, Jericho may have suffered quakes in antiquity that tumbled sections of its defensive walls, allowing entry by attackers.

emphasis on God's swift accomplishment of his purpose, and on the unassailable might that confirmed the rightness of his ways.

In 1925, the German biblical scholar Albrecht Alt had gone so far as to claim that there never had been a conquest. Instead, he suggested, the Israelites had been nomads who had penetrated slowly and peacefully into the hill country of Palestine, where there was room for them to settle. Alt was not an archaeologist, and his theory was based solely on detailed analysis of biblical texts and other documents. The crucial point he gleaned from these sources was that the rugged upland interior had had few Canaanite inhabitants in the period of the late Bronze Age, just before the Israelites apparently emerged. Thus, without displacing others, the Israelites would have been able to turn from pastoralism to settled farming over a timespan lasting probably several generations. Occasionally there would doubtless have been clashes with the inhabitants of the relatively crowded plains nearby, but only very gradually would the Israelites have acquired the strength to threaten the region's fortified city-states. Such later military forays could, then, have been the basis of the dramatic stories told in Joshua. Although Alt had conducted a purely textual investigation, discoveries in the field in the following decades did provide evidence to support his view, or at least to weaken the case for a Joshua-style string of conquests. In January 1952 the stage was set for a particularly critical challenge to the conquest model when the British archaeologist Kathleen Kenyon began work on Jericho, the most famous site of the Joshua period.

The fall of Jericho is one of the best known stories in the Old Testament. It certainly stands as the dramatic high point of the Book of Joshua. The early chapters recount how, from an encampment on the eastern side of the Jordan River, Joshua sends spies into Canaan, "even Jericho," to scout the territory and the city's defenses. Then, in an echo of Yahweh's parting of the

Tourists examine Jericho's massive 30-foot-high main defensive tower of rough-hewn stone, part of the oldest known fortifications on earth. Digs by Britain's Kathleen Kenyon (right) and others have found that the bottom section of the tower dates to 8000 BC and that the walls were reconstructed numerous times during the third millennium BC.

Archaeologist Kathleen Kenyon, who excavated Jericho in the 1950s, examines some of the plaster-coated and painted skulls with shells for eyes that she unearthed, evidence that the city's prehistoric people practiced some sort of worship of the dead 9,000 years ago.

Red Sea that delivered his people from the pursuing Egyptians, Joshua leads the children of Israel to the banks of the river, and "the waters which came down from above stood and rose up upon an heap . . . and those that came down toward the sea of the plain, even the salt sea, failed, and were cut off: and the people passed over right against Jericho." In obedience to the Lord's command, the Israelites then march around the city walls for seven days, and on the seventh, "Joshua said unto the people, Shout; for the Lord hath given you the city . . . and it came to pass, when the people heard the sound of the trumpet, and the people shouted with a great shout, that the wall fell down flat. . . . And they utterly destroyed all that was in the city, both man and woman, young and old, and ox, and sheep, and ass, with the edge of the sword."

Jericho has always been a special place. As the Jordan descends far below sea level toward the sterile waste of the Dead Sea, the fields and orchards of Jericho appear as a cool island of green amid the baked white desert that surrounds them. As Kenyon once wrote, "In this dazzling expanse, the oasis of Jericho stands rather as one imagines the Garden of Eden did in the account in the Book of Genesis." So it must surely have seemed to the first Israelites, as they approached the city from the barren land east of Jordan so many centuries ago. The miracle is entirely due to the city's ancient system of springs, which still supports the modern town and its agriculture. The original inhabitants apparently relied on one particular source, now known as Ain es Sultan; a venerable mound nearby, at the western edge of the oasis, testifies to long centuries of occupation in the area, and this was where Kenyon began digging.

There had already been several excavations on the Jericho tell. One, led by the British archaeologist John Garstang in the 1930s, had found the remains of a collapsed network of walls that had apparently fallen in dramatic fashion, rather than through neglect or natural decay over time. Garstang—who was backed by funding from the British conservative Sir Charles Marston, a staunch supporter of the notion that archaeology in the Holy Land was essentially about verifying the Bible—applied a convenient dating method and was soon able to declare that these were the very defenses brought down by Joshua. But Kenyon, hailed by many as one of the most distinguished archaeologists of her time, brought to the site more precise techniques, developed during the course of digs in her native Britain. These techniques, a refined version of methods first applied by Flinders Petrie a half-century before, depended on rigorous examination of the soil and very careful recording of its stratification. At Jericho, Kenyon dug a deep, relatively narrow trench from top to bottom of the whole sloping mound. By keeping the edges of the trench clean and squared off, she obtained a cross section of the city through its entire history. When wider areas had to be cleared—for example, to reveal the floor plan of a house—she dug down in measured squares, leaving an untouched strip between each section so that the stratification would remain visible.

Kenyon was intrigued by the Joshua story and the possibility of confirming or refuting it. But she was even more enthralled by the sheer antiquity of the city. Over the next few years, she focused on tracing the history of Jericho back to its earliest settlement. Trenching down toward bedrock, she found that the first walled city, with substantial houses and courtyards, had been constructed 10,000 or more years ago, in Neolithic times. In a tomb not far above the deepest layer, Kenyon was able to see something of the city's early inhabitants. The Jerichites, it seemed, had made cult objects out of skulls. At a level roughly equivalent to the seventh millennium BC, she found skulls that had been covered with molded clay and then painted—work, she wrote, "of extraordinary delicacy." She was convinced they were portraits, prepared from the remains of ancestors.

The Neolithic wall was only one of many that Kenyon unearthed. In the layers corresponding to the early Bronze Age—an 800-year span ending about 2300 BC—she found that successive ramparts had been repaired and rebuilt at least 17 times. The damage may have been caused by earthquakes. The most recent of these walls—dated by Kenyon to 2300 BC—had been misdated by Garstang to the 15th century (when he believed the Exodus had occurred), a period for which Kenyon could find no evidence of defensive structures whatsoever. In fact, her excavations demonstrated that after about 1350 BC, the site lay unoccupied for centuries. In short, there was simply nothing for Joshua to destroy.

More testimony against the conquest theory came from the Israeli archaeologist Yohanan Aharoni. In 1957 he examined a number of village sites in Galilee, not far from Hazor, and determined that they had first been settled before the destruction of the city. The villages were all small and unfortified, the kind of settlements that

ANGUISHED LETTERS TO PHARAOH

Cries from antiquity, the pair of small pillow-shaped clay slabs at right belong to the collection of 350 extraordinary missives—the so-called Amarna Letters—discovered at el-Amarna, site of the pharaoh Akhenaten's short-lived capital. Like the other letters, these were written by Canaanite rulers allied with Egypt who were desperately trying to maintain the pharaoh's power in Canaan during the chaotic 14th century BC. The one at the top was sent to Akhenaten by Tushratta, king of the Mitannians. The other, also full of complaints, was written by Yahtiri, governor of Gaza and Joppa.

Many of the Amarna Letters sound dire alarms. Subject peoples in the Near East were restless, especially the Apiru, or bandits, whom some scholars equate with the Hebrews, who had become chief troublemakers in the area. To some scholars this is evidence that the Israelites did not invade Canaan but rather were downtrodden natives violently asserting their rights.

The letters doubtless caused headaches for the pharaoh—and for his scribes. Written in cuneiform, the stylus-on-clay writing system common in the Middle East, they would have been incomprehensible to readers of hieroglyphs. The language used was Akkadian. Akhenaten must have employed translators to turn the letters into Egyptian and then translate the answers he sent back to his troubled vassals.

would likely have been built by a seminomadic people with little to fear from their neighbors. Sites investigated in the 1960s and 1970s followed the same pattern. Yadin never accepted Aharoni's dating, and the debate between them turned first rancorous, then vituperative. But Yadin, still clinging to the idea of an abrupt conquest, was in a shrinking minority. Most others found it more plausible to envisage the incoming Israelites as small, tribal bands, filling the empty places in the landscape wherever possible and frequently living side by side with the Canaanites.

Challenges to the Joshua account opened the door for more controversial theories. In 1962, the American biblical scholar G. E. Mendenhall came out with a shockingly radical concept. There had been no influx at all, he declared, neither violent nor peaceful, no Exodus from Egypt, and before that no patriarchs. He dismissed as romantic nonsense the whole idea of the nomadic Hebrews arriving from the desert with their cult of Yahweh. Instead, he said, the Hebrews had been in Canaan all the time—as the lower classes, the exploited, landless peasants who bore the burden of the city-state dwellers on their toiling shoulders. By the 13th century the peasants had had enough, and they rebelled against their parasitic overlords. First they withdrew themselves from the tightly organized urban economies; then—and only as necessary—they destroyed the cities themselves. According to Mendenhall, the Israelite attachment to Yahweh sprang into being in 13th-century Canaan as a political and social ideology, designed to give the rebels a passionate group solidarity and to replace the master-slave relationships of the state they had violently rejected with a new allegiance to a divine sovereign. Mendenhall's evidence, like Alt's before him, was primarily textual, involving a reference to a rebellious people that may have been the ancient Hebrews in a collection of 14th-century Egyptian clay tablets known as the Amarna Letters (*opposite*). But political events of more recent vintage provided an opportunity to check Mendenhall's theory against archaeological findings. After the 1967 Arab-Israeli war, the central hill country of Palestine came under the control of Israel. Subsequent research revealed for the first time the sheer magnitude of the settlement in this region at about the time that scholars agreed the Israelites had become a recognizable presence in Canaan. Surveys found 23 villages dating to the late Bronze Age; by the early Iron Age, just after 1200 BC, the number had risen to more than 300. That a major demographic change had occurred was obvious. However, archaeologists were hard-pressed to find any qualitative development, an observable alteration in lifestyle that would mark a divide between a Canaanite *before* and an Israelite *after*.

Of course, if Mendenhall's ideas were correct, no such cultural watershed would be expected. His peasants'-revolt hypothesis hinged on the idea that Canaanite and Israelite were one and the same. This was, at best, negative evidence and could prove nothing, but the post-1967 surveys did reveal some aspects of the village life of the period that were at least compatible with the theory. Houses were approximately equal in size, with four banks of rooms and a courtyard, rock-hewn water cisterns and grain silos. There was thus no sign of any social hierarchy among the villagers, and fragments of writing that turned up relatively frequently suggested a fairly high level of literacy. Both factors seemed to match Mendenhall's picture of politically conscious rebels in a breakaway society.

Rebels or interlopers, the people of these settlements lived very simply. They had little or no furniture, making do with stone benches built in along the base of interior walls. Families apparently slept together in the largest room, with nothing more than a mat to serve as a bed. Cooking fires were set outside the front door or in an open courtyard shared by several households. Despite the relative poverty, most villages had metalworking equipment for casting and repairing bronze and some iron tools.

The remains of these communities could never furnish real proof of Mendenhall's theory, but the concept of Israel as a revolutionary Canaanite antistate was at least plausible, and to some scholars deeply attractive. Among the most controversial of these was the American academic Norman Gottwald, who took up the cause in the 1970s. He attempted to explain not only the emergence of what he called "liberated Israel" but also the principles of Yahweh worship in terms of a modified Marxist sociology. Some rejected his approach out of hand as mere polemics, although

A collection of plain pottery vessels used by early Israelite settlers in their hill-country villages in central Canaan at the end of the 10th century BC includes tall 10- to 15-gallon jugs with collars around the rims, probably for storing water in the dry, inhospitable land. Later, after they had acquired iron tools, the Israelites were able to dig cisterns in the rock beneath their settlements and had less need for the large containers.

Complete with a neatly fitted lid, a Canaanite cosmetic box of ivory carved in the shape of a duck reveals the sophistication of artisans working in the comfortable cities of Canaan. The box—apparently inspired by an Egyptian prototype—was fashioned about 1350 BC.

his exhaustive, 900-page book on the subject struck others as a masterpiece of carefully reasoned, if laborious, analysis.

Not surprisingly, Gottwald's thesis inspired counterarguments from many scholars, including the Israeli archaeologist Israel Finkelstein, who in the 1980s directed one of the most extensive surface surveys of the hill-country sites at the crux of the debate. Socioliterary perspectives were all very well, reckoned the veteran fieldworker, but archaeology and ecology should come first. The 300 or so supposedly early Israelite settlements that he and his colleagues had examined are situated mostly on the highland frontier, relatively far from the large Canaanite urban centers. Finkelstein argued that the founders of these communities were not refugees from the cities, as Mendenhall and Gottwald had contended, but pastoral nomads from the local countryside. Echoing Albrecht Alt's theory of peaceful infiltration by outsiders but with a more local flavor, he maintained that these wanderers had relocated and become sedentary stockbreeders and farmers at a time when the longstanding Canaanite culture of the Bronze Age was beginning to totter and about to give way to new Iron Age peoples and ideas.

The debate may never be settled in favor of any one of these hypotheses over the others. Many scholars have concluded that Israel's rise to prominence, like so many cultural and political developments throughout history, was a decidedly complex affair. In fact, the three main theories are by no means mutually exclusive, and a combination of all three probably explains the events of the 13th and 12th centuries best. After all, someone burned Hazor and at least a few other of the cities supposedly conquered by Joshua; there are clear signs of long cohabitation between the region's different groups; and city-state peasants were undoubtedly oppressed. It is not too hard to imagine a largely peaceful migration into Canaan, in which an Israelite marauding party might grasp at the occasional opportunity to seize, loot, and burn an established community. And in such a time of change and confusion, it is not at all improbable that the Israelites were supported by Canaanite dissidents who eventually came to share the Yahweh worship of their allies and were ultimately absorbed into their community. As for the Exodus itself, archaeology has remained essentially silent, although there is evidence that some Hebrew peoples did live in Egypt in the years preceding Israel's emergence in Canaan. If nothing else, the central role of the story in the faith of the Jews offers eloquent testimony that some sort of seminal event along the lines of the well-known biblical account was part of the early history of the Israelites.

Whatever their origins, the Israelites in Canaan appear to have maintained a distinctively egalitarian, theocratic society for the best part of two centuries, a legacy that would carry forward and have important influences on the development of Western civilization. Their political structure was summarized in the last verse of the Book of Judges: "In those days there was no king in Israel: every man did that which was right in his own eyes." For Mendenhall and Gott-wald, it was a golden age of political liberty. But golden or not, the social experiment would soon be interrupted, in part because of internal difficulties, but also because of external pressures. Another people was moving into Palestinian history. As Judges put it, "And the children of Israel did evil again in the sight of the Lord; and the Lord delivered them into the hand of the Philistines forty years."

Ancient texts give a rather one-sided view of the Philistines. Because they were the oppressors of Israel for so long and its dire foe in many battles, the Bible excoriates them as murderous idolaters and arrogant bullies; Egyptian records refer to them as thieves and pirates. Even in modern times, their name has been appropriated as an epithet for oafs and anti-intellectual boors. The Philistines themselves remain frustratingly silent: No writings of theirs have ever been discovered. Modern archaeology, however, has helped to redress the imbalance. Various sites in the Holy Land have revealed that the Philistines developed one of the most brilliant civilizations of their time. Their story, had it ever been recorded, would probably have formed as epic a tale as the biblical account of the Israelites' own adventures. They were one of the so-called Sea Peoples, part of a great Bronze Age migration across the waters of the Mediterranean, driven by the social chaos created as the advanced cultures of the Aegean crumbled into a long dark age. Some sailed as far as Sardinia; others headed to the rich coastal lands on the Mediterranean's eastern shore.

Relic of the Philistine invaders of Canaan, a rhyton, or drinking cup, is incised with the face of a stylized, amiable lion. The cup was used in a shrine at Ekron, a large city between Jerusalem and the Mediterranean Sea that was a center of the advanced culture the Philistines brought with them when they fled from the upheavals racking their original home in the Aegean region.

Testament to the skill of Philistine potters, an artful jug, painted in red and black with birds, fish, and other motifs, boasts a spout with a built-in strainer to catch the dregs of wine or beer.

The biblical Philistines reached the eastern Mediterranean in the early 12th century BC, not long after the Israelites had become a force to reckon with in the region. Almost at once, they ran into serious—and well-documented—resistance. Pharaoh Ramses III, who died in 1151 BC, had his mortuary temple decorated with scenes of a great land-sea victory over the incomers along the Canaanite coast, close to the Egyptian frontier, which probably took place about 1175 BC. According to papyrus documents as well as the great carved relief on the temple, Egyptian forces swooped upon the Philistines, trapping them "like birds in a net." In the aftermath, Ramses' chronicle relates, "the Philistines were made ashes."

It was hardly a battle between equals. From the scenes on the relief, it appears that the Egyptian troops launched a surprise attack on an entire refugee nation. Most of the Philistines were marching along the coast, their women and children in oxcarts, while their fighting ships kept pace close inshore. Even with the encumbrance of their dependents, however, Philistine spearmen, chariots, and vessels probably gave a good account of themselves. The battle was almost certainly not the devastating success that the pharaoh claimed; far from reducing them to ashes, the Egyptian ruler permitted the Philistines to settle permanently on the very coast he had supposedly swept them from, one of the region's most fertile areas. Furthermore, a vigorous Philistine defense would not have been particularly surprising: The Aegean world at the time, despite its political difficulties, was a center of high technology, and the immigrants brought with them not only traditions of sophisticated urban living but also the new skill of iron smelting and the powerful weapons it enabled them to make.

Ramses' concession has often been taken to mean that the Philistines were allowed to remain in Canaan only as sworn vassals, or at least as mercenary fighters, of the

Bronze rivets still fix a corroded iron knife blade to its ivory handle with pommel and suspension hole, made by a Philistine craftsman about 1150 BC. Among the first people to master the forging of iron weapons, the Philistines harried the Israelites for almost two centuries and defeated them in several battles before being pushed back by resurgent Hebrew forces into their own cities near the Mediterranean coast.

pharaoh. It is at least as likely that the relief is simply an indulgence in ritual boasting, a common practice among the ancient Egyptians. More likely still is the probability that the Ramses relief disguises an Egyptian defeat, at best a defensive draw, on the borders of the pharaoh's kingdom. The coming of the Philistines coincided with a temporary end to Egypt's increasingly fragile lordship over Canaan, and in fact was probably the actual cause. At various excavated sites along the southwestern coast of Canaan are clear signs of destruction in the late 13th or early 12th century, with an abundance of Aegean-style, Philistine-made pottery appearing in the layer dating from immediately after the destruction. The archaeological record also reveals a mid-12th-century Egyptian withdrawal from centers they had previously occupied in the region.

According to the Bible, within a generation or two the Philistines had built five linked city-states of their own, all on or near the Canaanite coast: Ashkelon, Ashdod, Gaza, Gath, and Ekron (the actual situation was probably more complex). Subject people or not, they were Canaan's most powerful residents, and a formidable enemy for the people of Yahweh. Thanks in part to their high-technology weapons, the Philistines were able to inflict punishing defeats on the Israelites, culminating in the capture of the Ark of the Covenant itself, which they hauled in triumph to Ekron: "And the Philistines fought, and Israel was smitten, and they fled every man into his tent: and there was a very great slaughter; for there fell of Israel thirty thousand footmen. And the ark of God was taken." They maintained control not least because of their near monopoly on ironworking facilities, as the rueful words of the First Book of Samuel make clear: "Now there was no smith found throughout all the land of Israel: for the Philistines said, Lest the Hebrews make them swords or spears."

Although the Bible acknowledges some of the grand works of Israel's hated enemy, the full extent of Philistine achievements remained largely unknown for more than 3,000 years. But starting in the 1960s, Israeli archaeologists turned their attention to some of the most famous sites. A particularly rewarding investigation got under way in the 1980s, when a joint Israeli-American expedition started digging into the ruins of ancient Ekron. It had at one time been a powerful fortified city on the border between Philistine and Judean territory, strategically placed near the main road to Egypt. Now it

was a dusty 50-acre mound known as Tel Miqne, forgotten amid the cotton fields of a thriving kibbutz; to explore it, the expedition even had to build its own road.

The results of the excavation were startling. "It was as though we were opening a time capsule," reported the American codirector, Seymour Gitin. "All we had to do was to brush off 10 centimeters of topsoil." The team soon found great quantities of superb pottery they first assumed to have been imported from the Aegean. When researchers subjected sample potsherds to a modern procedure known as neutron activation analysis—a method of measuring minute quantities of trace elements, whose proportions differ subtly from clay source to clay source—they discovered that the Ekron ware had been made from Canaanite raw materials. Gitin's Israeli colleague Trude Dothan soon unearthed the kilns in which the pottery had been fired, as well as an area of the city that appeared to have been set aside for such industry, well away from residential sections. She also discovered traces of metalworking equipment and the rusted remnants of some finely wrought iron knives. These were the earliest pieces of smelted iron ever found in the region; older examples, discovered in Egypt, had all been worked from iron meteorites.

Battling to unite the various regions inhabited by the Israelites, King David—in an etching by Gustave Doré—drives a fearsome chariot that impales enemy troops during his victory over the Ammonites. Responding to his triumphs, the southern and northern tribes selected David as their king.

The dig also brought to light the remains of a splendid architecture—buildings that exemplified a fusion of Aegean, Egyptian, and Canaanite styles. Some scholars have since speculated that the Philistines may well have been responsible for the introduction to the Middle East of the squared, dressed stone blocks known as ashlars. Ekron's structures included a vast, skillfully designed edifice covering almost 2,300 square feet, the largest Philistine building ever found in the region. It may have been a temple or a palace, containing both an altar and a large, Aegean-style central hearth. Cult figures of Canaanite gods, found side by side with the Philistines' own, suggested that they had absorbed at least some of the local religious traditions.

Life in such a city would have been reasonably comfortable, with running water, good sanitation, plentiful oil lamps, and a vast array of household utensils. The evidence from Ekron indicates that the Philistines served as a kind of bridge between the Aegean world and the cultures of their new homeland, a vital and highly influential link between West and East. Despite the bitter enmity that would eventually arise between them, in the early days the Philistines' more advanced society had assuredly impressed and affected their Israelite neighbors, who endured a much rougher existence. For perhaps a century, the two peoples lived together without major warfare, the Philistines in the fertile plains and the Israelites in the harsher, more marginal uplands. But sometime around 1080 BC, in the period covered by the First Book of Samuel, the Philistines were ready to begin their attempted takeover of the hill country, too, and the great clash began. It would bring with it a marked change among the Israelites, who were initially incapable of holding their own against such a powerful opponent. As the Bible documents, the struggle first for survival and then for military victory transformed the egalitarian Israelites of Judges into the monarchic Israel of Kings.

The Bible presents the clamor of the Israelites for a king-commander as a falling away from the ideals of Yahweh. The prophet Samuel castigates them with these blistering words: "And ye have this day rejected your God, who himself saved you out of all your adversities and tribulations; and ye have said unto him, Nay, but set a king over us." The chosen candidate was Saul, of the tribe of Benjamin, and as a war leader, he was a failure. At the disastrous battle of Mount Gilboa, he died with his sons and most of his men at the hands of a Philistine army that was simply beyond the ability of the Israelites—with their obsolete bronze weapons—to defeat.

Saul's reign was marked by incessant quarrels with religious leaders. On the surface, this denoted a certain amount of unrest in the society, but it was in essence a demonstration of a fundamental characteristic of this people. Although they would turn again and again to the secular solution of kingship, their strength lay in the spiritual relationship they had forged with their God—a relationship that they would continually renew through the agency of prophets and other moral leaders. In the end, it is their veneration of the divine law of Yahweh, rather than of any human authority, that supports them through their travails. The point comes through even more clearly in the familiar story of Saul's ultimate successor, David. He enters the biblical narrative in heroic fashion—the young shepherd boy who, armed only with a sling, destroys the Philistine giant, Goliath. His career thereafter swings back and forth from ignominy to nobility, impressing upon the reader that even the greatest of warriors and charismatic commanders cannot escape his inherent human frailty. David is, finally, the quintessential Old Testament character: made not of mythic stuff but of real flesh and blood.

The Bible has few stories to match David's, beginning with his rise to the position of King Saul's lieutenant, Saul's growing jealousy of his able subordinate, and David's subsequent fall from royal favorite to outlaw. For more than a year he served as a mercenary with Israel's Philistine enemies, gaining training and experience that rounded out a natural talent. After the death of Saul, it was his military ability that led the southern tribes, the tribes of Judah, to choose him as their king, initially, it seems, with Philistine support; soon afterward, he was separately elected king of the tribes of the north. It was the beginning of the United Monarchy, a period that would see Israel rise from a tribal society to a major regional power.

But there was unfinished business to attend to first. The Philistines remained undefeated, still terrifyingly powerful, while David's double kingdom and its potential resources were still divided by a tract of territory held by the Canaanites. To this hostile wedge he now turned his attention. One city in particular was the key to the whole strategic situation: a fortified town set squarely on the ridge that was the only practicable north-south route through the hill country. The city was called Jerusalem, and the story of Israel's kingdom would be written there.

In 1990, Harvard University's Leon Levy Expedition to the ruined Canaanite city of Ashkelon, on the Mediterranean coast of present-day Israel, was in its sixth summer of digging when it made its greatest find to date. Poking from the earth was the small (four and a half by four inches) bronze bull calf pictured above, still bearing traces of its silver plating. Around the figure lay pieces of the pottery shrine that had once contained it.

This was plainly no ordinary sculpture, but a rendering of the divine mount on which, the Canaanites believed, their most important gods rode. It was also, of course, a "graven image"—of the kind forbidden to the Israelites. In the Bible, Moses castigates his Hebrew followers for worshiping a golden calf, then grinds the calf to powder, mixes it with water, and makes them drink the liquid. Lawrence Stager, the expedition's leader, proposes that the Israelites were, in fact, a Canaanite offshoot, who condemned calf worship and

other Canaanite customs as one way of differentiating themselves from such idolaters.

The Ashkelon calf, the third such image discovered in Israel and the oldest, had been buried under rubble during an Egyptian attack in about 1550 BC. At that time Ashkelon was already ancient—a thriving seaport almost 2,000 years old with some 15,000 inhabitants. For another 2,500 years it would remain a center of trade and culture, controlled by a succession of vibrant peoples. After the close of the Canaanite era, the city passed through Philistine, Phoenician, Roman, Byzantine, and Muslim hands before undergoing major destruction in AD 1191, during the Crusades.

Where Ashkelon's earlier excavators, Britain's Lady Hester Stanhope in 1815 and John Garstang in 1920 and 1921, barely scratched the surface, Stager and his team dug deep. In the process they sliced through 20 strata of successive occupation and assembled a picture of life in Ashkelon down through the ages.

A SECURE WALL FOR THE CANAANITE CITY

One of the Harvard team's big surprises was how extensive Ashkelon was. Garstang in 1920 had estimated that the population had crowded into a settlement of only 15 acres; the city, in fact, turned out to be 10 times that size.

One of the largest and richest of Mediterranean seaports, Ashkelon was protected within a mile-and-a-half arc of earthen ramparts (below). These huge city walls, rising more than 50 feet, sloped outward to a base 75 feet thick. They were filled with layers of soil and sand, and their angled faces, or glacis, were of fieldstones covered with mud plaster. A deep trench, perhaps a moat, dug to bedrock where possible, ran along the outside. The glacis' peculiar construction, Stager believes, was a Canaanite invention to defeat one of the era's most powerful methods of siege warfare—tunneling. Any tunnelers would have had to start their digging on the other side of the trench, making them visible targets. And even if they had been able to bore through the walls, they would have been smothered by the loose fill pouring down on them from within.

Inside the fortifications, the Harvard team found Canaanite graves equipped with food and other goods for use by the dead in the next world (opposite). Many of the items had been imported, confirming Ashkelon's importance as a center of trade in the ancient world

The city became an object of Egyptian wrath after the Hyksos who were possibly a Canaanite dynasty, were driven out of Egypt where they had ruled. The Egyptians forced the Hyksos into Canaan, and Ashkelon fell under Egyptian sway, except for one brief revolt in 1207 BC. A decade or two later, when Israelites and Philistines attacked, burned, and occupied many Canaanite cities, the last vestiges of Egyptian and Canaanite dominion over Ashkelon vanished

Excavation of Ashkelon's north rampart exposes various historical layers. A Hellenistic wall (top left) *stands above a Philistine mud-brick tower; the Canaanite Sanctuary of the Calf is at the base.*

The grave at right yielded these scarabs, carved in the stylized and symmetrical Egyptian Hyksos style, as well as pottery (bottom) *imported to Ashkelon from Syria and Cyprus. One bowl still held the remnants of food offerings* (bottom right). *The Cypriot jugs, decorated with a poppy design, may have contained opium.*

A student volunteer and a staff member excavate the skeleton of a young Canaanite woman at Ashkelon. The corpse was buried within the city, in a vault lined with mud bricks. These practices, and the grave goods (above and below) *laid beside her, helped researchers date her death fairly precisely at about 1500 BC.*

Ashkelon under the Philistines, from the 12th to the 7th century BC, was the detested Ashkelon of the Hebrew Bible. In this era, it was one of the city-states of the Pentapolis, whose kings the Book of Joshua calls "five lords of the Philistines." Enmity between Ashkelon and Israel is recorded in 2 Sam. 1:20, as David mourns the death of Saul, the Israelites' king: "Publish it not in the streets of Ashkelon," he warns, "lest the daughters of the Philistines rejoice, lest the daughters of the uncircumcised triumph." The hatred was mutual: The Bible credits the Philistines with being master metalworkers but says they refused to divulge their skills to the Israelites.

The Bible sheds no light on when the Philistines came to Ashkelon, or from where. Pottery finds, however, have led Stager to theorize that the Philistines were Mycenaean Greeks who settled in the city around 1175 BC, after losing a great battle to the Egyptians.

Although the term *philistine* has come to mean "coarse and uncultured" in modern times, this reflects less an objective appraisal of this ancient people than it does the enmity of their declared foes, the Israelites. In fact, recent archaeological discoveries have shown that the Philistines were, by the standards of the time, an advanced society in terms of wealth, artistic development, and standard of living. Their pottery, for instance, was finer than contemporary Israelite wares.

Philistine tenure in Ashkelon came to an end in dramatic fashion in 604 BC, when the Babylonian army under King Nebuchadnezzar razed the city, nearly 20 years before he laid Jerusalem to waste. Nebuchadnezzar took many captives into exile in Babylon, where the Philistines lost their ethnic identity. In time, only the name Philistia—later, Palestine—clung to the region the Philistines had once dominated.

A lone excavator probes the floor of a 12th-century BC public building used by Philistines for weaving. Discoveries included examples of two closely linked styles of local pottery (opposite).

Feathered headgear distinguishes these captive Philistine soldiers in a relief carved for the pharaoh Ramses III. Ramses defeated the Philistine army and the so-called Sea Peoples in about 1175 BC.

Pottery decorated with two colors, like the bowl at right, was long regarded as typical of the Philistines. Stager suggests that although the earlier monochrome ware, represented by the bowl above, was decorated in Mycenaean style, it was not an import but was made of Ashkelon clay and thus also Philistine. If he is right, this identifies the Philistines as Mycenaeans and places their earliest appearance in Ashkelon around 1175 BC.

The Persians, who overcame Babylonia in the sixth century BC, added the territories of the Holy Land to their empire. But rather than rule in Ashkelon themselves, they put the city under the benign leadership of neighboring Phoenicia.

Excavating one seaside warehouse dating from this period (*right*), the archaeologists came upon amphorae for shipping wine and olive oil, Phoenician silver coins; and artisans' raw materials, such as bone and pigments. But a surprise awaited them in the debris and sand that covered the floor—a dog cemetery, the largest yet found in the ancient world. After the warehouse fell into disuse, the site became a burial place for the animals. Stager theorizes that, since dogs lick and heal their own wounds, these animals were part of a healing cult, similar to ones that flourished in Greece and Mesopotamia.

Ashkelon endured as power in the region passed from the Persians to Alexander the Great, then to the Ptolemies of Egypt and the Seleucids of Syria. In the second century BC, when Jewish armies burned and sacked nearby cities, Ashkelon made peace and was spared. Coins minted by the city in the first century BC bore this inscription: "Of the people of Ascalon, holy, city of asylum, autonomous." Once again Ashkelon survived, to reach even greater prosperity under Rome.

The ruins of a warehouse are part of an occupational deposit 10 feet thick built up during the 200-year-long Persian period. The round shaft (foreground) was sunk by the 1921 archaeological expedition

A pottery vessel in the shape of a blowfish was made in Ashkelon during the Persian period, but in Phoenician style. The Harvard dig found a strong Phoenician influence in objects produced during the Persian period, but scant trace of Persian sensibilities.

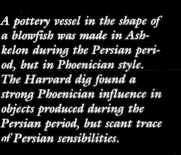

Skeletons of a puppy and a female dog lie on their sides with their tails tucked around their hind legs. More than a thousand dogs, all carefully interred, were excavated from the warehouse pictured opposite. Since the bones were free of any marks of injury, the zoarchaeologists who examined them concluded that the animals were not sacrificed or butchered for food but died naturally.

Two religious icons (right) attest to Ashkelon's cultural diversity in the Persian era. The skirted bone cutout represents Tanit, a Phoenician mother goddess; the crowned bronze figurine is Osiris, Egyptian god of the dead.

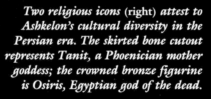

The owl gazing from this two-handled cup is the symbol of Athena, patron goddess of Athens. The vessel, made near Athens in the fifth century BC and excavated from the warehouse opposite, is evidence of Ashkelon's trade with Greece.

No mere colony but a "free and allied city" of the Roman Empire, the great port of Ashkelon enjoyed both commercial and intellectual prominence during the Roman era. The city grew through the generosity of the new king of neighboring Judea, Herod, who endowed Ashkelon—some say because he was born here—with marketplaces, public baths and gardens, and a palace for the Roman emperor.

Evidence of these extensive works—documented by the Jewish historian Josephus—has yet to turn up. In 1921 Garstang uncovered a large colonnaded assembly hall and mistook it for a peristyle of Herod's; further examination of both the site and its statuary dates the structure two centuries later, to the reign of the emperor Severus. Other Roman-era ruins unearthed in Ashkelon include a sunken theater, a painted tomb *(detail, opposite, top left)*, and a patrician house that held a collection of erotic lamps. Ashkelon's long history came to an end during the Crusades, that bloody struggle between Christian and Muslim nations for control of the Holy Land. Ironically, it was not the Christian invaders but the Muslim defenders, under Saladin, who leveled the city, along with other ports, to weaken the Crusaders' sea advantage.

"Ashkelon was a town likable to the heart," wrote one Muslim observer sadly of its devastation, and Saladin's decision "was a very painful thing for him. He said, 'I would rather be bereaved of all my children than destroy a single stone of it. But if God foreordained anything, it is bound to be carried out.'" And so, for 10 days in September of 1191, "the Sultan and his sons," along with his army, "exerted themselves tremendously in ruining the town," toppling ancient towers, burning the houses, and choking the harbor with uprooted Roman columns.

Nike, Greek goddess of victory, stands on a globe supported by Atlas in this statue dating from about AD 205. With a twin, it flanked the doorway of a basilica excavated by Garstang in 1921.

This one-inch token, made of bone turned on a lathe, served as a gaming piece or a ticket to a play in a Roman theater in Ashkelon. The abbreviated skyline shown on one side, an insignia or logo for the city, reappears in later mosaics.

A boy bends over a basket of grapes in this detail from the ceiling of a tomb decorated late in the Roman period. The painting depicts the wine feast held after death in Greek mythology.

A detail from a marble sarcophagus (below) that was unearthed by a bulldozer at a construction site depicts battling Greeks, Trojans, and Amazons.

JERUSALEM: THE DREAM AND THE NIGHTMARE

A fragment of a terra-cotta figure from an incense stand found in Jerusalem and dating to the 10th century BC, when the heroic King David made the city the Israelite capital, shows a bearded man clutching the legs of an animal he carries on his shoulders.

One dark night in April 1911, a small band of Englishmen disguised in Arab dress slipped into the mosque known as the Dome of the Rock. Sitting like a golden crown atop the Temple Mount in the heart of old Jerusalem, the shrine covered one of Islam's holiest places, the rock from which Muhammad was said to have ascended on his night visit to heaven to meet Moses, Elijah, and Jesus. Here, too, according to Jewish tradition, Abraham had prepared to offer up his son Isaac as a sacrifice.

But the intruders had not come to marvel at hoofprint-shaped hollows in the stone, supposedly cut by the Prophet's horse as he took his skyward leap, nor to contemplate the spot where Isaac had walked free and Abraham received Yahweh's blessing. Theirs was a quest for something far more tangible and, in their view, more glorious: the hidden treasure of King Solomon's Temple.

According to old, persistent legends, this hoard of sacred objects, wrought of the purest gold and silver, had been concealed by Temple priests in 586 BC as the Babylonian king Nebuchadnezzar sacked the city. In 1908 Valter Juvelius, a Swedish scholar and self-styled "master philosopher," claimed that he had decoded a cryptic segment of the Book of the Prophet Ezekiel that revealed the treasure's hiding place. The prize lay in a cave deep inside the Temple Mount, reachable only by a secret passage. All Juvelius needed, he declared, was money to finance an expedition. Investors could be sure of fabulous rewards.

Montague Brownslow Parker, a 30-year-old English aristocrat, took up Juvelius's cause. Fresh out of the Grenadier Guards and hungry for adventure, Parker used his social contacts with the English upper class and wealthy Americans to bankroll the project. Among the subscribers he managed to entice were the duchess of Marlborough and the Chicago Armours, of meat-packing fame.

Expenses would be high. At the time, Palestine lay under the control of the Ottoman Empire, which claimed ownership of any antiquities found within its territories; hefty bribes would thus be required to buy the cooperation of local officials. Parker himself made little effort to hold down costs, spending freely on excavation equipment and to fit out a yacht to convey himself and a few friends from England to the Palestinian port of Jaffa. He also arranged for luxurious accommodations at his headquarters on the Mount of Olives, staffed by a team of chefs and other domestic attendants.

Once in Jerusalem, Parker was careful to publicize the enterprise as a general archaeological expedition rather than a tightly targeted treasure hunt. To deflect the skepticism of excavators already at work in the city, who looked with scorn and some dismay upon this foray led by obvious amateurs, he hired a leading authority on the archaeology of Jerusalem—the Dominican scholar Père Louis

Hugues Vincent—to serve as a consultant. Tempted by the generous budget, Vincent seized what he considered was an unprecedented opportunity for scientific investigation, apparently remaining innocent of Parker's true intentions.

For more than two years, Parker sought the hidden passageway, exploring the shafts of the ancient water-supply system first probed by Charles Warren in 1867. Despite expert help from tunneling engineers who had worked on London's new underground railway—and from a Danish clairvoyant recruited by Juvelius—Parker dug in vain.

The Turkish authorities eventually lost patience. In the spring of 1911, Parker was given a strict time limit of only four months to complete his work and clear out.

The young Englishman grew desperate. He felt sure that he would find the treasure if only he could excavate a particular section of the Temple Mount. But the spot lay within the precincts of the Dome of the Rock, which by a centuries-old decree could be entered only by Muslims. Risking wrath and retribution, Parker offered bribes to two of the area's highest-ranking officials, the Ottoman governor of Jerusalem and Sheik Khalil, hereditary guardian of the mosque. The gamble paid off: They agreed to allow what amounted to the ultimate sacrilege—a clandestine excavation into holy ground.

To conceal their identity, Parker and his team donned Arab

In this modern view of Jerusalem, the gleaming top of the Muslim shrine, the Dome of the Rock, dominates the hill where King Solomon built his Temple. Below the Temple Mount lies a large excavated area; to the left, outside the walls, can be seen another dig on the ridge south of the Old City where David established his capital 3,000 years ago.

robes and headgear, and worked only at night. On April 17, they descended a stairway under the great rock itself and lowered themselves by ropes into a subterranean chamber. On the cavern's floor, a slab of stone covered a mysterious depression known to Muslims as the Well of Souls. Jewish folklore as well as Islamic legend suggested that a cache of precious objects lay beneath it.

Soon after midnight, the men's pickaxes bit into the stone. But within a few moments they had to stop. A mosque attendant, knowing nothing of the covert arrangements made by the sheik, chanced to enter the sanctuary and surprised the Englishmen at their work. Aghast at this act of desecration, he rushed into the streets to raise the alarm.

The town was overflowing with pilgrims: Muslims gathered for the feast of Nebi Mussa, Jews observing Passover, Christians celebrating Easter. As news of the attendant's discovery spread, rumors flew. One story had it that the foreigners had found and made off with the Ark of the Covenant; other voices claimed the prize had been King Solomon's crown, or the fabled sword of Muhammad. The Muslim crowds were particularly incensed, and turned their fury on Sheik Khalil and the Ottoman governor. They were accused of complicity, mobbed and spat upon. In the chaos that followed, Parker and his comrades managed to slip away to the port of Jaffa and sail for home—empty-handed but glad to escape with their lives.

Leader of a rogue expedition to Jerusalem between 1909 and 1911, Captain Montague Parker, who dreamed of finding—and taking—the fabled buried treasures of King Solomon, sits wearily in a tunnel laboriously cleared by his excavating team. Parker believed the tunnel would lead to a secret passage under the Dome of the Rock (right) and thus to the treasure he thought was worth $200 million. Caught inside the shrine's forbidden precincts, he and his partners were forced to flee for their lives.

Although present-day archaeologists are infinitely more professional and more cautious than Parker, digging in Jerusalem still holds its dangers. A city continuously inhabited for more than 5,000 years, home to mutually suspicious peoples and sacred to three religions, where virtually every step treads on holy or historic ground, can hardly be other than a minefield.

In 1981, for instance, the distinguished Israeli archaeologist Yigal Shiloh reaped a whirlwind during his excavations on the hill of Ophel—a rocky 15-acre spur extending southward from the Temple Mount. Local ultraorthodox Jews, convinced that the site was a medieval Jewish cemetery, stormed the dig, hurling stones and curses at the workers for their disturbance of the dead. Politicians representing the fundamentalist interests lobbied the government to bring a halt to Shiloh's work. The whole nation was swept into the controversy, which the Israeli press dubbed the War of the Bones. Even-

cense; he often neglected to write up his finds and acquisitions adequately. In his defense, the argument has been made that much of what he found would have otherwise gone unnoticed or been destroyed by developers. And though he refused to lay down his shovel, he once invited government officials to help themselves to anything they wanted—whereupon they seized half his cache.

Compounding the controversy, Arab workers tended to contact Dayan rather than the proper authorities when they chanced upon a find. On one occasion, a farmer bulldozing near Gaza uncovered an ancient burial ground; it was Dayan he called—and to whom he sold 23 mummy-shaped coffins containing the remains of Egyptians serving under Ramses II.

For Dayan, who shrugged off his critics, the objects were a link to his homeland's rich past. "It is these ordinary articles," he said, "that provide the bond, intimate, personal, with the world of antiquity, a world that has fallen silent but has not vanished." Today his collection is housed in Jerusalem's Israel Museum.

prayers would mention it, and pilgrims would brave the dangers of the road to climb its steps at great annual festivals; adult males would be required to present themselves for worship there three times a year. The hills of Jerusalem would ring with the music of the Temple's harpists and cymbal players, and the smoke of animal sacrifices would drift in the air, wafting skyward to "make a sweet savour in the nostrils of Yahweh."

The building of this shrine—part of a complex of courts, royal residences, and ceremonial palaces—consumed the king's attention for at least seven years. Phoenician laborers and craftsmen were hired to help with the work, and an ambitious earthmoving project got things under way. The top of Mount Moriah, where the Dome of the Rock now rises, was leveled to provide a platform, and massive blocks of stone were hoisted into place for the walls and floor. Basic engineering problems were compounded by the insistence—on the part of the king and his priests—that no sound of chisel, hammer, or other iron tool defile the aura of sanctity within those holy precincts. Archaeologists studying the remnants of other structures from the same era have proposed that the builders solved the problem by using prefabricated panels of dressed stone or wood, prepared and decorated at some other location, then conveyed in silence to their proper places.

If base metals were unwelcome on the premises, their nobler counterparts most certainly were not. Those inner walls not paneled with cedar or covered with carvings of plants and fantastical beasts were lined with sheets of purest gold; sacrificial altars and giant basins were wrought of burnished bronze.

Of all this architectural grandeur, however, not one stone has been found. In fact, despite the efforts of generations of investigators, no direct archaeological evidence of the First Temple's existence has ever surfaced. The destructive vengeance of the city's subsequent conquerors, or perhaps the zeal of its rebuilders, may have eradicated every trace of Solomon's great shrine. Its wonders survive only in the written word of Scripture.

One small physical link to Solomon's Temple did eventually come to light, at a time when archaeologists were beginning to despair of ever finding any tangible clues to this great period in Jerusalem's history. In the summer of 1979, the French biblical scholar André Lemaire wandered into the shop of an antiquities dealer in Jerusalem and was offered the chance to examine a small ivory pomegranate, no larger than a thumb. On it was a fragmentary inscription in ancient Hebrew characters. Lemaire was later allowed to photograph the object, and after some study came up with a plausible reading, since corroborated by other scholars: "Belonging to the Temple of Yahweh, holy to the priests."

Probably filched by a workman from a nearby archaeological site, the tiny fruit appeared to be a relic from the time of Solomon's Temple, but researchers were unable to confirm this for a number of years. For some reason, Lemaire could not get the antiquities dealer to produce the pomegranate again, and it completely disappeared for six years. Somewhere during that time, it was apparently smuggled out of the country, showing up in Paris at an exhibition in 1985. Through a series of secret deals, it was subsequently bought by the Israel Museum and returned to Israel in 1988, where it was finally subjected to paleographic analysis and chemical tests. The results were unequivocal: This was no forgery, but an artifact labeled by the hand of a scribe working in the late eighth century BC, when Solomon's Temple still stood.

Throughout the ancient Near East, the pomegranate had been a popular decorative motif, as well as a symbol of fertility. According to the books of Kings and Chronicles, chains of carved pomegranates adorned the two bronze columns that guarded the entrance to Solomon's Temple. Instructions set down in Exodus detailed that the high priest's ceremonial robes were to be hemmed with a band of "pomegranates of blue, and of purple, and of scarlet . . . and bells of gold between them round about."

Despite the commanding presence of the Temple and its priests, not everyone in Jerusalem pinned their faith on Yahweh alone. There were some—possibly women seeking any and every form of talismanic defense against the perils of childbirth—who treasured ceramic female figurines bearing a marked resemblance to the old Canaanite mother goddesses. In a cave on the eastern slope of the Ophel, Kathleen Kenyon found in the 1960s what she described as a "veritable cascade" of these and other ceramic objects strongly suggestive of a heretical cult, including an incense burner and statuettes of horses with

Solomon's Temple crowns the Temple Mount at right in a re-creation of ancient Jerusalem. In the middle—supported by the stepped-stone buttress—rise a palace complex and government citadel; dwellings huddle inside the great walls at left. Also shown is Jerusalem's vital water-supply system fed by the Gihon spring, outside the main gate at center. From it water flowed through a conduit into the city to a storage pool at far left, and through a channel with several openings to irrigate the fields below the walls.

Thought to be the only relic of Solomon's Temple ever found, a pomegranate—just two inches high—of lustrous ivory carries an inscription in the ancient Hebrew alphabet that was used by the Israelites only before the Temple's destruction by Babylonian invaders in the early sixth century BC. The carving, with its four remaining petals, may have decorated a priest's scepter or an altar.

what seemed to be solar symbols on their foreheads. They dated from a period some generations after Solomon and reminded Kenyon of an episode narrated in the Second Book of Kings, when the reforming king Josiah sought to stamp out pagan practices in his realm: "And he put down the idolatrous priests . . . them also that burned incense unto Baal, to the sun, and to the moon. . . . And he took away the horses that the kings of Judah had given to the sun. . . ."

Such heresies may only have been minor aberrations, but one way or another the great capital of Solomon and his successors flourished for some 400 years in the shadow of his Temple. Jerusalem was by far the most important and wealthiest city of the region, at least 10 times the size of Lachish, the second-largest urban center. Just before and during the reign of Hezekiah, who ruled from 715 to 687 BC, events in the world beyond caused Jerusalem to grow even more extensive. In 722, the Assyrian king Sargon conquered the 10 northern tribes of Israel, who had previously separated themselves from Solomon's Judean kingdom to form a state of their own. Refugees who escaped death or slavery sought shelter in Jerusalem, and the city swelled beyond its previous boundaries. In anticipation of a siege by Sargon's son Sennacherib, Hezekiah extended the city's defenses to the west, enclosing the new settlements behind a massive rampart (as well as ensuring the city's water supply with the underground aqueduct rediscovered by Edward Robinson in 1838). He may have also been responsible for the imposing 25-foot-high watchtower uncovered by Nahman Avigad in 1975, which was girded by a wall of hard, unhewn stone some 12 feet thick.

A SUBTERRANEAN CITY WONDROUSLY PRESERVED IN THE JUDEAN FOOTHILLS

One of the the most dramatic Holy Land discoveries of recent times occurred at the site of the once-thriving Edomite settlement of Maresha, southwest of Jerusalem. As long ago as 1900, British archaeologists unearthed its walls and found several layers of dwellings that revealed that Maresha had been built and destroyed and built again three times between 800 and the last century BC. Then, in 1980, the archaeologist Amos Kloner, director of the Israel Antiquities Authority, digging in the commercial portion of the city, came upon a vast series of labyrinthine caves beneath Maresha, unrivaled in their complexity anywhere else in the ancient world.

Beginning about 2,800 years ago, the inhabitants dug the caves in the soft limestone that lay only a few feet beneath their streets and houses. There in the underground coolness, protected from the broiling summer heat by a natural form of air conditioning, hundreds of the city's 5,000 inhabitants labored in workshops, stored their goods, stabled their horses. Here they also raised huge flocks of pigeons in multistoried dovecotes, using the birds for food and the droppings for fertilizer. Most important, they made olive oil in the caves. No fewer than 20 stone presses have

been found, enough to supply the needs of Maresha and have enough left over to export at least 190 tons each season.

All this activity effectively came to a halt in 113 BC when the Maccabean John Hyrcanus conquered the Edomites. But the ghostly cave city, hidden safely below ground from plundering humans and ravaging winds, survived virtually intact, packed with the best-preserved artifacts of ancient Judea ever discovered.

Two views of a roomy cave at Maresha show its neatly hewn steps and limestone walls and an olive press. Olives to be crushed for their oil were placed in the trough of the heavy lower stone, while workers rolled the circular grinding stone around the trough with the aid of a timber thrust through the hole.

Used as a dovecote, a cave with a 30-foot-high ceiling—now equipped with modern lighting—has rows of niches carved in its chalky walls to house the pigeons. At one period in the city's history, people raised about 100,000 of the birds at a time in 60 underground coops.

As Shiloh, Avigad, and others uncovered the remnants of Jerusalem in the days of the First Temple, they began to learn the names, and something of the day-to-day business, of its inhabitants. Many different artifacts—including storage jars whose handles were imprinted with owners' labels, official inscriptions, and religious dedications, as well as seals originally attached to long-vanished bundles of papyrus documents—have helped break the silence of the rubble heaps and tumbled stones that are so often all the city's excavators have to work with.

During a dig on the Ophel begun in 1980, in a terrace below the stepped-stone structure of David's reign, Shiloh found a room containing 51 of the clay seals known as bullae, which had originally been affixed to important documents. All but 10 bore legible inscriptions, and some still carried the marks of the rolled papyrus and binding strings that had once been attached to them. The names on the seals were typical of those of the sixth or seventh century BC, as known from the Bible and other ancient texts. Many, expressing a piety that was either heartfelt or merely conventional, included the suffix *yahu*—a reference to the Israelite name of God, Yahweh. There was, for example, an Ahiyahu (my brother is God) and a Benayahu (son of God). But for Shiloh, the most exciting of all was the bulla bearing the name of a person who appears more than once in the Book of Jeremiah—a scribe named Gemaryahu, son of Shaphan, employed in the royal court of King Jehoiakim around the end of the seventh century BC. It was one of very few instances in the history of Holy Land archaeology of a direct link between a specific person in the Bible and an actual relic. Gemaryahu himself may very well have stamped his name into the bulla's wet clay.

Ironically, the seals' state of preservation was itself testimony to an ancient disaster. The lumps of clay had been baked hard by a vast fire burning out of control. The room where they were found contained a large stockpile of arrowheads. The residents of Jerusalem were preparing to defend their city: Not long after the time of Gemaryahu, the tyrant Nebuchadnezzar of Babylon was on the march.

In 586 Nebuchadnezzar besieged Jerusalem. It took the better part of two years for him to starve out the inhabitants. At the base of the stout tower that had probably been built by Hezekiah, Nahman Avigad found four arrowheads, buried in a thick layer of ash from the burning

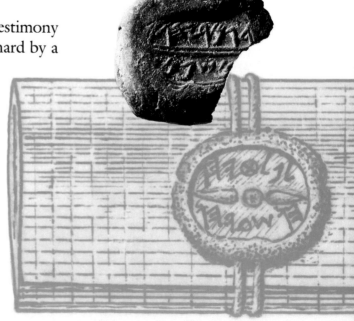

city and dust from its collapsing walls. Once the city's defenses were breached, the invaders wasted no time, putting the royal palace and the Temple to the torch. The realm of David and Solomon had plunged into darkness.

The biblical account gives the impression that Jerusalem was comprehensively laid waste by Nebuchadnezzar, its entire population massacred or marched off into exile—"And them that had escaped from the sword carried he away to Babylon"—and that only a few peasants were allowed to remain in the hinterlands, to plow fields and tend vines, presumably for the benefit of the occupying army. But the archaeological record tells a slightly different story, as the Israeli excavator Gabriel Barkay found out during his 1979 investigation of burial caves above the Valley of Hinnom—specifically the unlooted tomb made famous by his discovery of the two tiny silver scrolls inscribed with the priestly blessing from Numbers.

Evidence suggested that these communal tombs, each intended to house the bones of several generations of a single family, dated from the First Temple period. More significantly, however, analysis of the contents of the one cave that had been preserved intact indicated that it had remained in continuous use for several centuries, well past the time of Nebuchadnezzar's invasion.

In addition to the two precious scrolls and scattered human remains, Barkay found a vast repository of grave goods—more than 1,000 items in all—that testified to the wealth of the family that had owned the tomb. The hoard reflected the changing materials and methods of craftsmanship employed in the Near East and throughout the Mediterranean world from the eighth to the fifth century BC: ceramic wine jugs, perfume containers, and oil lamps; an Assyrian-style sarcophagus of a type rarely found in Judea; bone handles and ivory inlays; alabaster; tiny glass flasks made by a rare technique of

One of the 51 bullae (left)—half-inch-wide lumps of clay used to seal documents—that were found by Yigal Shiloh bears the actual imprint of the scribe Gemaryahu mentioned in the Old Testament. The drawing below indicates how a rolled papyrus scroll was wrapped with strings, which were then fastened with bullae stamped with such information as who the scribe had been.

the sixth and fifth centuries rendered obsolete by the introduction of glassblowing; beads of rock crystal, agate, and carnelian; earrings of gold and silver, encrusted with decoration and shaped into crescents, boats, or clustered fruits, following fashions seen as far afield as Sardinia, Etruria, and Spain.

Most poignant of all was a collection of metal arrowheads, dated to the time of Jerusalem's fall. The darts were bent or broken, suggesting that they had actually been used in battle. Barkay speculated that their owners may have been among those who fell in defense of the city and were buried here by their grieving kin. In any event, the evidence of the tomb made clear that a significant Jewish presence had never completely disappeared from the city. Barkay and his team concluded that certain of the items in the cave could have been produced only during the half-century of the Babylonian exile, indicating that at least one wealthy family had continued to conduct burials in the family sepulcher throughout the period; they were unlikely to have been the only upper-class Jews to remain.

As had happened many times before, the shifting politics of the region ensured that even mighty Nebuchadnezzar's empire would collapse, as it did in 539, falling to the Persians. Their king, Cyrus, allowed the descendants of those Jews who had indeed been exiled to return to their homeland as a subject people. When they returned—carrying the gold and silver vessels that had been plundered from the Temple but that Cyrus had restored to them—they brought new customs and spoke a different language. They still prayed in Hebrew, but the exchanges of their daily lives and businesses were now in Aramaic, another Semitic tongue.

Little archaeological evidence survives from the period immediately after the exiles' return. The burned-out shell of the Temple may have been used for sacrificial offerings, but the work of restoring it to its former glory proceeded only in fits and starts. According to the Bible, the prophet Haggai excoriated his neighbors for rebuilding their own homes before they attended to the house of the Lord. Shamed by this attack, two prominent members of the community— Zerubbabel, son of the governor of Judah under the Persians, and Joshua, son of the high priest—applied themselves to the task of reconstruction. Zerubbabel made use of remaining segments of the old walls and platform, adding new masonry where necessary. Some of his work is still visible along the eastern wall of the Temple Mount, where a straight joint marks the boundary between his layers of heavy, irregularly shaped stones and the smoother, more uniform blocks added in the next reconstruction, some 500 years later.

Despite these efforts, Jerusalem languished in a sorry state for many years. Now a minor provincial outpost rather than an independent capital, the city had no need for a palace and insufficient wealth even to clear away the debris of its earlier devastation. But by the middle of the fifth century, Judea had regained a small measure of autonomy, once more minting its own coins—albeit with the blessing of its Persian masters.

In 445 BC Nehemiah, a Jewish courtier serving the Persian ruler Artaxerxes, gained his sovereign's permission to rescue Jerusalem from decay. With letters of safe-conduct from the king, he traveled to Judea to survey the wreckage. Because he knew that there were those within the empire who opposed his plan, he carried out his work discreetly, under cover of darkness.

The farther he went, picking his way around the tumbled walls, the more depressing Nehemiah found the prospect. There were places where the paths were so choked with debris that his mount could not find a foothold. Nevertheless, he marshaled his forces, confounded those who jeered at him, and organized the heads of families and leaders of clans to put their backs into the project, assigning each group a specific section of the wall to repair or a new gate to erect, complete with all necessary bolts and bars. In due course, Artaxerxes made Nehemiah the province's governor, and from this position of power he encouraged large numbers of former exiles to return to their ancestral homeland and its capital.

King Herod's majestic new Temple of white marble partly plated with gold gleams in the middle of the vast complex of buildings constructed by the Roman-appointed king in the last decades before Christ. Doubling the size of the Temple Mount platform, Herod added a huge columned pavilion, the Royal Stoa, at the southern end, a bastion called the Antonia Fortress at the other, and surrounded the complex with massive walls, some more than 160 feet high, pierced with monumental gateways.

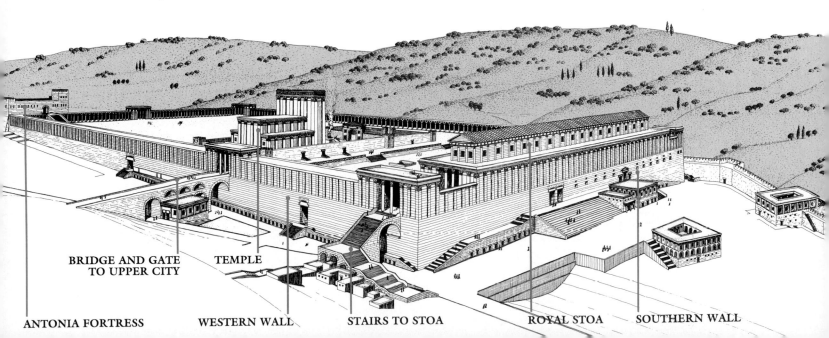

BRIDGE AND GATE
TO UPPER CITY

TEMPLE

ANTONIA FORTRESS

WESTERN WALL

STAIRS TO STOA

ROYAL STOA

SOUTHERN WALL

In its turn, the Persian Empire too came to an end. In 333 BC Alexander the Great seized control of the Near East. When he died, barely a decade later, his generals were left to split the geographic spoils, and Judea became yet again a pawn in a complex political game. In the third century BC, it was dominated by the Ptolemies, Egyptian rulers of Greek origin who had turned themselves into the final dynasty of pharaohs; by the second century, Judea's new overlords were descendants of the general Seleucus, who had become kings of Syria.

During this long period of cultural confusion, a rift developed between those Jews who adhered strictly to the laws of Moses and those who felt themselves drawn to the brave new cosmopolitanism of the Greeks. The Seleucid king Antiochus IV saw in the quarrel an opportunity to further his own political ends. In 169 BC he attacked Jerusalem, demolished its walls, burned many buildings, and raised a fortress in the heart of the city. According to the Jewish historian Josephus, writing in the first century AD, Antiochus deliberately placed the citadel so that it looked down upon the Temple as a deliberate affront to its priests. Not stopping there, he banned all worship of Yahweh, substituting the cult of Olympian Zeus and setting up a sacrificial altar to that god within the Temple itself.

Pushed too far, the Jews rebelled two years later. Led by Judah Maccabee, a member of the priestly Hasmonean family, the uprising escalated into a drawn-out struggle for independence. The Temple was recaptured in 164, but it would be another 20 years before the Hasmoneans stormed Antiochus' fortress and liberated the whole of Jerusalem. Their first act was to extend, rebuild, and reinforce the city's defenses. The Jews were again lords of the land, but their freedom would last barely 100 years.

The heirs of the Hasmoneans turned themselves into kings, and their dynastic quarrels led to a breach that soon spelled disaster. In 63 BC, John Hyrcanus II summoned outside help to support him in a bitter fight against his brothers. The Roman general Pompey, extending the Roman Empire to the Near East, was only too happy to accept the invitation. His troops arrived as mediators but remained as occupiers. By 37 BC, Judea had become a client state of imperial Rome, ruled by a puppet monarch.

102

Rome's choice, known to history as Herod the Great, was not regarded as truly Jewish by many of his subjects. His forebears were Edomites, an Arab people only lately converted to Judaism; to the truly orthodox, who disapproved anyway of his Hellenistic outlook and deference to Rome, he remained an alien. But to others, he was an advocate of Jewish interests in the court of the only superpower of the age. Whatever his motives, he accomplished what none of his predecessors had: the rebuilding of the Temple at Jerusalem.

Josephus, who saw the finished edifice, recorded Herod's announcement of his intentions. At one time a provincial governor himself, Josephus may have copied the speech from the royal archive, perhaps adding a few embellishments, since his own political survival—like Herod's—depended upon his loyalty to Rome. "The enterprise that I now propose to undertake," declared Herod to an assembly of Jewish elders, "is the most pious and beautiful of our time." He did not forget to acknowledge the cooperation of his Roman sponsors: "Since, by the will of God, I am now ruler, and there continues to be a long period of peace and an abundance of wealth and great revenues, and—what is of most importance—the Romans, who are, so to speak, the masters of the world, are loyal friends, I will by this act of piety make full return to God for the gift of this kingdom."

Although only the foundation stones of Herod's Temple complex remain, documentary sources have preserved virtually every facet of its construction and decoration, down to the dimensions of its drains. Josephus gives detailed descriptions in two of his surviving works, *Jewish Antiquities* and *The Jewish War;* the scion of a priestly family, he would know well of what he spoke, most likely having grown up in the shadow of the shrine.

The Temple was 11 years in the making: 8 years for masons to quarry, dress, and transport the great stone blocks, each weighing somewhere between 2 and 10 tons; and 3 more years for the extension of the original Temple Mount into a great platform measuring 1,575 feet on its longest wall, and for the construction of the Temple itself. So holy was this final task that it was performed solely by initiated priests. Aspects of the work not requiring the same degree of ritual purity were carried out instead by some 18,000 laborers.

Benjamin Mazar (top), *director of a massive dig in the vicinity of the Temple Mount, sits amid the ruins of a royal administrative building near the Mount's southern wall, while excavation supervisor Yacov Nadelman writes up an account of the day's finds. Mazar's decade-long investigation attracted volunteers from all over the world.*

A dramatic relic found by Mazar's colleague Meir Ben-Dov, the broken stone at right has an inscription reading, "To the place of trumpeting." It probably marked a niche on the Temple Mount parapet where priests sounded the shofar, or ram's horn trumpet, to announce the beginning and end of the Jewish Sabbath. It fell into the street below when Roman legionaries demolished the entire Temple complex in 70 AD.

The size of the actual sanctuary was restricted by religious law to the modest dimensions of Solomon's original shrine. Herod compensated with a spectacular new setting for the sacred site: retaining walls nearly 100 feet high to support the enlarged Temple Mount, a broad esplanade, imposing portals, blocks of multicolored marble, and a facade covered with plates of gold.

The effect was dazzling. "Whoever has not seen Jerusalem in her splendor," said one admirer, "has never seen a lovely city. He who has not seen the Temple in its full construction has never seen a glorious building in his life." "To approaching strangers," recalled Josephus, "the Temple appeared from a distance like a snow-clad mountain; for all that was not overlaid with gold was purest white."

Once within the sacred precincts, worshipers could nourish their souls and feast their eyes on ornaments worked in precious metals and colored stone. Roman writers of the period, such as Tacitus and Florus, corroborate Josephus' description of a massive golden vine, dripping with clusters of golden grapes—each bunch as large as a man—that hung over the door to the sanctuary. The entrance was veiled with a curtain of Babylonian tapestry, richly embroidered in symbolic hues—scarlet for fire, light brown for earth, blue for the air, and purple for the sea.

Inside the sanctuary, the mingled smoke of 13 different kinds of incense rose from a golden altar, and seven lights glowed from the seven branches of the Menorah, the sacred lampstand that illuminated the entrance to the Holy of Holies. Into this last chamber none but the high priest could enter, and he himself could do so only on the Day of Atonement, the holiest day of the year.

After long centuries, the children of Israel again looked to the Temple as the earthly embodiment of their faith. On the High Holy Days of autumn, and during the other great festivals of the Jewish calendar, pilgrims poured into Jerusalem to worship there. The city's permanent population during Herod's reign has been estimated at 150,000 to 200,000, boosted in the course of the year by an influx of as many as 100,000 visitors.

For the city authorities, the management of this traffic was a perpetual nightmare. Modern excavators, exploring the perimeters of the Temple Mount, have found evidence of how Herod's engineers sought to mitigate the problem. In 1968, the Israeli archaeologists Benjamin Mazar and Meir Ben-Dov launched a systematic 10-year excavation of the areas immediately to the south and west of the Mount, during which they were able to revise the theories of earlier investigators about the purpose of certain structural remains.

For instance, after his pioneering survey of 1838, Edward Robinson had postulated that a fragmentary arch he discovered jutting from a section of the western wall had been part of a bridge spanning the Tyropoeon Valley and leading to the Upper City. But there was no sign of supporting piers for the rest of the bridge. Probing an area slightly to the south, Mazar and Ben-Dov came upon the foundations of other supports lying at right angles to the direction of the hypothesized bridge. They realized that the so-called Robinson's Arch had actually been part of a monumental L-shaped staircase providing access to the southern end of the Temple Mount from a main street running along the valley floor.

Mazar and Ben-Dov also proposed a solution to the mystery of Barclay's Gate, named for the British architect J. T. Barclay, who had discovered the feature in the middle of the 19th century. Barclay and others had been puzzled by the gateway's position in the western wall, opening at a height that would have been inaccessible from the main street of the valley. But Mazar and Ben-Dov's research suggested that the gate was at the level of a second, upper thoroughfare running along the western wall. This elevated passageway, reached by short stairways from the main street, provided an alternative route for visitors entering or leaving the holy precinct. Furthermore, it was supported by vaulted chambers tucked

up against the base of the western wall, housing shops that probably served the throngs of pilgrims. Within the rubble, the excavators found scattered some of the many coins visitors spent here.

No matter how lively the crowds or how heavy the press of pilgrims, there came a moment in every week when the frenzy stopped. Josephus recounted how, from the top of a tower rising above the chambers of the priests, at the southwestern corner of the Temple Mount, "it was the custom for one of the priests to stand and to give notice, by sound of trumpet, in the afternoon of the approach, and on the following evening of the close, of every seventh day, announcing to the people the respective hours for ceasing work and for resuming their labors."

While probing at the foot of the Temple Mount walls, Ben-Dov and his colleagues unearthed a stone from the topmost corner of this tower, identified by a fragmentary inscription as belonging to the place where the Sabbath trumpet had actually been sounded. The missing part of the inscription may have included the name of a donor who had contributed to the cost of the stone or, perhaps, subsidized the construction of the entire tower. Among those Jews blessed with worldly wealth, such endowments were regarded as a pious obligation.

Although their Temple has vanished, some of the homes of Herod's subjects still remain, buried beneath the streets of present-day Jerusalem. In excavations begun in 1969 in an area of the Old City known in modern times as the Jewish Quarter—just to the west of the Temple Mount—Nahman Avigad unearthed several commodious houses dating from the Herodian age that reveal much about the lives and tastes of their occupants. The floor plan of one such dwelling covers more than 2,000 square feet. In this and other spacious residences—one of which is known popularly as the Mansion—wealthy Jerusalemites enjoyed a way of life similar to that of the upper classes throughout the Roman world. They decorated their walls with frescoes colored and figured in the popular Hellenistic style, trod on floors tiled with handsome mosaics, dined at tables with stone tops, and brightened their homes with all sorts of finely wrought objects. One of the most elegant pieces recovered by Avigad was a green fluted pitcher of blown glass, signed

These parts of a colorful mosaic once belonged to the floor of the inner court of an elegant house in the old Upper City of Jerusalem, home to wealthy Jews during Herod the Great's reign. Also found during excavations by Nahman Avigad in the 1960s and 1970s were the remains of a painted stucco ceiling (top) *and a wealth of stone furniture and stone vessels for food and drink* (left and above).

in Greek letters by its maker, Ennion, a craftsman known to have been at work in neighboring Phoenicia during the first century AD.

But a visitor from any other Hellenized city in the Roman Empire would have found something alien about these otherwise cosmopolitan homes. There were no statues of nymphs or pagan deities, no fountains spouting from the mouths of mythological creatures. A Jewish family might choose—as did the occupants of one excavated dwelling—to ignore the religious ban on drinking wine made by non-Jews, stocking their cellars with the products of favored Italian vineyards, but most households gave every sign of adherence to the laws of ritual purity.

Food was often cooked and served in vessels of stone, which, unlike ordinary pottery, could not be contaminated or rendered unclean according to Jewish dietary laws. At one site, excavators found a cistern filled with ceramic vessels that had been deliberately pierced and broken, possibly because some forbidden contact, such as milk and meat in the same dish, had rendered them unfit for use. And almost every house contained at least one small pool for the ritual immersions required for men before the Sabbath and for women during the days of menstrual bleeding.

Among the families who lived in this part of the city was at least one who was not only rich but who also stood high in the ranks of the theological hierarchy. Avigad's excavators found an inscription identifying one of the dwellings as the property of the priestly clan known as the House of Kathros. It was a dynasty with an unfortunate reputation, immortalized in Talmudic writings for some act of bureaucratic tyranny or corruption: "Woe is me because of the House of Kathros, woe is me because of their pens."

But for the power hungry and the pious alike, the presence of Herod's Temple loomed large. Its own glorious contours and those of attendant buildings atop the grand platform of the Temple Mount were inescapable features of the view from almost every residence in the city. Enduring features, however, they were not to be. Within 75 years of his death in 4 BC, Herod's great masterwork would lie in ruins, and further turmoil would await. For Jerusalem and the Holy Land, where a new religion that would irrevocably alter the future of the region was about to spring to life, neither the dream nor the nightmare was close to being over.

Although it was winter, a glaze of heat shimmered on the limestone cliffs fringing the Wadi Qumran, the dry riverbed that winds down to the northwest shore of the Dead Sea. Fatigued by his hot climb up the steep escarpment, Muhammad adh-Dhib—a Bedouin boy of the Tamireh tribe that ranged this stark sliver of the Judean wilderness—paused to survey his surroundings. Hoping to scare up his lost goat, Muhammad tossed a stone into a crevice in the cliff. But instead of a bleat, he heard the clink of shattering pottery. Intrigued, he clambered up to the narrow opening (*shown enlarged above*) and peered inside. Lining the back of the dim recess were several earthen jars. A faint, rank odor met his nose. Suddenly fearful, the shepherd boy reeled and fled, his goat forgotten.

The next day, Muhammad returned to the cave with a friend and wriggled into the chamber. Round about stood seven jars. Upending several of them, the treasure seekers found nothing but pebbly debris. Secreted in another, however, were three curious leather bundles wrapped in decaying linen. Gingerly, they stashed these crumbling curios in a sack, and—seeing no evidence of valuables—quickly departed.

Though they could not have known it at the time, the moldering parchments they toted from the cave that afternoon in 1947 would prove to be priceless finds—sacred writings (*background*) from an ancient Jewish library that had been hidden in the honeycombed cliffs of Wadi Qumran almost 1,900 years earlier. The story of how these Dead Sea Scrolls made their journey from the Qumran caves to the desks of biblical scholars is as convoluted as any street map of old Jerusalem. Circulated through seedy antique shops, brooding monasteries, and high-security bank vaults, bartered and sold in clandestine encounters, the scrolls would unleash a whirlwind of debate about the nature of the Bible and the origins of Christianity and modern Judaism that continues to this day.

In spring 1947, suspecting that the peculiar manuscripts might be salable, two Tamireh Bedouins took the scrolls to Bethlehem to the shop of cobbler and sometime antiquities dealer Khalil Iskander Shahin, a Syrian Orthodox Christian who went by the nickname Kando. The wily Kando, sensing their value, quickly offered to broker their sale. His efforts to locate a suitable buyer led him to Saint Mark's in Jerusalem, a repository of rare manuscripts. The Jacobite monastery's ecclesiastical leader, Metropolitan Athanasius Yeshua Samuel, at once recognized the scrolls' antiquity and agreed to buy any other scrolls Kando could lay his hands on. But Kando demurred. He knew he must be careful—dealing in improperly acquired archaeological treasures could get him in trouble. Moreover, in these, the waning days of the British mandate, travel in and about Jerusalem had grown hazardous.

To Samuel's distress, Kando remained incommunicado for some time. Then, in July, Kando dispatched three Bedouins to Saint Mark's to show the metropol-

Desolate repository of the Dead Sea Scrolls, the forbidding cliffs of the Wadi Qumran were uninhabited from Roman times until the arrival of Bedouin in the 17th century. Visible on the left are entrances to Caves 5 and 4. Cave 4, which proved to be the richest depository, is seen in closeup below.

110

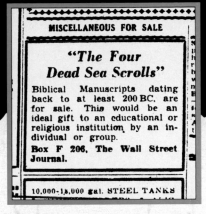

The broken halves of the copper scroll below list 64 secret locations of some 200 tons of gold and silver and other valuables, perhaps from Jerusalem's Temple. The inventory, etched in colloquial Hebrew, remained unread until scientists devised the technique of coating the brittle scroll in plastic and slicing it into thin strips.

Unassumingly tucked between "Business Opportunities" and "Real Estate," this Wall Street Journal *advertisement caught the eye of an Israeli journalist in 1954.*

itan the three original scrolls again, along with four more they had discovered. When the ragged band reached Saint Mark's clutching their disintegrating parchments, the monk at the gate—who had not been told to expect them—turned them away. Before Samuel knew what had happened, the shepherds had returned to Bethlehem, and one, in a pique, sold his scrolls to a Muslim sheik. Kando quickly bought the remaining four and sold them to Samuel.

In an effort to determine the nature and exact age of the scrolls, Samuel contacted the head of Hebrew University's Department of Archaeology, Professor Eleazar Sukenik. Unbeknown to Samuel, Sukenik already possessed three Dead Sea Scrolls—no doubt the same three that had slipped through Samuel's fingers. In November 1947, on a tip from an Armenian antiques dealer, Sukenik had journeyed through Arab Jerusalem to Bethlehem to view the scrolls. Having mortgaged his house to help raise the necessary funds, Sukenik bought the manuscripts and, concealing them in a brown paper bag, returned home. The next day, the United Nations sanctioned the creation of the State of Israel. For Sukenik, the almost-simultaneous purchase of the sacred scrolls and the rebirth of a Jewish homeland constituted a divine coincidence.

Determined to also have the metropolitan's scrolls for Israel, Sukenik met with Samuel later that winter. But Samuel had already struck a bargain with the American Schools of Oriental Research to authenticate and photograph three of the four scrolls. In January 1949, persuaded that the manuscripts would fetch a high price in the United States, Samuel smuggled them aboard a plane bound for New York. Almost immedi-

ately he set about finding a buyer, but largely because his legal title to the scrolls was contestable, he had no takers. Finally, after five years of frustration, Samuel placed an anonymous advertisement in the June 1, 1954, *Wall Street Journal*.

It was then that another of the quirks of fate that seemed to govern the scrolls' progress came into play. Sukenik's son, Yigael Yadin—a doctoral candidate in archaeology at Hebrew University—happened to be in New York. When an Israeli journalist based in the United States called his attention to the ad, Yadin acted. Realizing that the Syrian Samuel would not deal with a Jew, he organized an elaborate deception. He arranged to have a New York banker respond to the ad, and then asked the distinguished philologist Dr. Harry Orlinsky to verify the scrolls' authenticity under the pseudonym of Mr. Green. Through his intermediary, Yadin purchased the coveted scrolls on July 1, 1954, for $250,000. Not until February 13, 1955, however, did Israel announce its remarkable acquisition.

Archaeologists G. Lankester Harding (foreground) *and Father Roland de Vaux sit among the ruins of the Qumran complex and sort through a basket of rubble. A clay jar identical to those found in the nearby caves was unearthed here.*

While the drama of Samuel's quest for a wealthy patron was playing itself out in America, another of greater proportions was unfolding in Qumran. In November 1948, G. Lankester Harding, director of the Department of Antiquities for Arab Palestine, belatedly read of the discovery of the Dead Sea Scrolls. Aghast that such finds had taken place without government involvement, Harding sprang into action. Within two months, using every scholar, sleuth, and desert guide at his disposal, the resourceful director had discovered the location of the original cave. Shortly thereafter, Harding was able not only to win the confidence of Kando but also to drive a bargain with the Tamireh, who henceforth were to bring all their finds to the Palestine Archaeological Museum, for which they would be paid.

Although Harding continued the search, most dis-

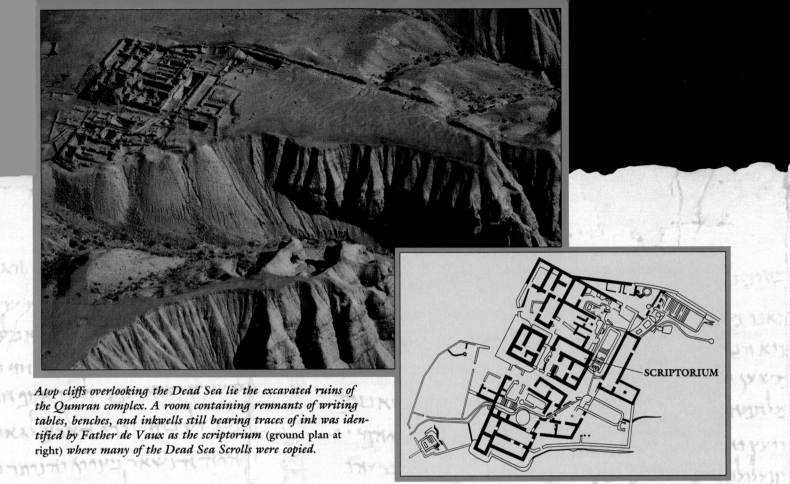

Atop cliffs overlooking the Dead Sea lie the excavated ruins of the Qumran complex. A room containing remnants of writing tables, benches, and inkwells still bearing traces of ink was identified by Father de Vaux as the scriptorium (ground plan at right) where many of the Dead Sea Scrolls were copied.

SCRIPTORIUM

coveries were made by the Tamireh, for whom scroll hunting became big business. In spring 1952, dismayed at the Bedouins' growing monopoly on finds, Father Roland de Vaux, director of the French-Catholic École Biblique, and William Reed, director of the American Schools of Oriental Research, began a systematic exploration of the Qumran cliffs, examining hundreds of crevices in which ancient parchments could have been deposited, and locating 37 caves that contained pottery and other traces of human habitation. This was punishing work: As excavators probed their way through centuries of debris, dust coated their eyes, noses, and throats, and clung to every find. But their efforts were to be rewarded, for in the so-called Cave 3, de Vaux and his team uncovered a one-of-a-kind copper scroll listing the locations of hidden treasure—perhaps the fabled wealth of the Temple of Jerusalem.

All discoveries paled beside those of Cave 4, however. In it, buried under six feet of bat dung, lay fragments of more than 500 scrolls. Though excavations

would continue for another four years, yielding more than 800 documents from a total of 11 caves, no other single site would prove so bounteous. Taken together, the scrolls constituted a vast library containing several copies of every book of the Old Testament except Esther; numerous Bible-like books attributed to biblical heroes or written as supplemental devotional texts; and a smaller number of doctrinal, legal, and messianic writings apparently penned by a little-known sect of Jews.

De Vaux purchased one lot from Cave 4, discovered by Bedouins, for $3,600. The ravages of time had reduced the scrolls to 75,000 pieces. To deal with this windfall, the museum convened an international team of seven scholars in 1952. Under the leadership of de Vaux, the all-Christian team would take until 1960 to clean and arrange the fragments for further study.

While the seven scholars struggled to impose order on the unruly mass of documents, de Vaux was sorting out another mystery: who had owned the scrolls. In 1951, he had begun excavating a site on the plateau

YIGAEL YADIN

KANDO

Joseph Shenhav and Ruth Yekutieli of the Israel Museum use tweezers to piece together scroll fragments, part of a parchment wad that tore away from the main document. Said archaeologist Yadin of their condition, "Letters and even words had peeled off some of the columns of script and attached themselves, in mirror image, on the backs of preceding columns."

The clean, spare script of the Temple Scroll shows through tissue-thin parchment, nowhere more than four-thousandths of an inch thick. Wrapped in cellophane and a towel and buried for years inside a shoebox, the manuscript suffered moisture damage that transformed one end into a fudgelike goo.

above the Qumran cliffs. By 1956, a large complex containing what de Vaux took to be a scriptorium, or copying room set aside for scribes, a communal dining hall, a kitchen, an assembly room, workshops, and extensive waterworks had been uncovered. No living quarters were found, suggesting that the inhabitants dwelled in the adjacent caves or in tents.

Aided by historical accounts by the Roman scholar Pliny and the Jewish historian Josephus, de Vaux worked with clues from the site itself as well as with those offered by the scrolls. He concluded that the mysterious ruins had been the center of an obscure sect known as the Essenes—one of three ideologic movements of Palestinian Jewry around the first century AD. From their writings emerged the portrait of an ascetic,

pacifistic people who believed in predestination and who cherished hopes of imminent apocalypse.

The fate of the Essenes is uncertain. De Vaux, who surmised that the Essenes were the caretakers of the scrolls as well as the authors of some of them, believed that they fell victim to invading Romans in AD 68, and that before they perished, they stashed their precious library in the nearby caves to save it from destruction.

In 1956, as de Vaux's work on the Qumran ruins drew to a close, the Bedouins discovered a final cache of well-preserved scrolls concealed behind a rock slide in Cave 11. Five found their way to the museum; at least two others, however, were rumored to have passed into private hands. For four years, scholars harbored hopes that another ragtag shepherd would appear, sacred documents up his sleeve. None came.

In 1960, Yigael Yadin received a letter from an American clergyman—dubbed Mr. Z—who offered to arrange the sale of a Dead Sea Scroll to Israel. A flurry of correspondence ensued, in which Mr. Z—ostensibly

One of the longest scrolls, the Temple Scroll, is 27 feet in length and contains 66 columns. The column on the left begins a discussion of the royal prerogatives and responsibilities of the king of Israel. Interesting, in the scroll "I" is used for "Lord"; thus God speaks directly to his people.

representing a Jordanian antiquities dealer—quoted Yadin a price of $1 million. Yadin countered with an offer of $130,000. Mr. Z conveyed Yadin's offer to the anonymous dealer, who, as it turned out, was none other than Kando. Surprisingly, the hard-bargaining antiquary assented to the sale.

As a token of good faith, Yadin forwarded $10,000 to Mr. Z. By then, however, Kando had reneged, disappointed not to have received full payment. His asking price rebounded to $1 million. Mr. Z, now angry, brashly tore off a piece of Kando's scroll. Reasoning that an actual fragment of the manuscript might move him to increase his offer, Mr. Z took the scrap to Yadin, who was on sabbatical in London. Coolly, he studied the piece and declared that it was nothing but a land deed. Mr. Z retrieved his bit of scroll and departed. Yadin saw neither Mr. Z nor his $10,000 again.

Although he had no direct proof, Yadin deduced that Kando had been Mr. Z's Jordanian contact. In 1967, after Bethlehem came under Israeli control as a result of

the Six-Day War, Yadin, who also served as general adviser to Prime Minister Levi Eshkol, saw his chance to obtain the elusive scroll and dispatched an army officer to Kando in Bethlehem. Under coercion, Kando lifted floorboards and produced a worm-eaten parchment, which the officer took to Yadin.

In 1977, Yadin published a three-volume, 900-page work on the scroll. According to him, the document presented itself as a book of religious law given on Mount Sinai by God himself and written down by the founder of the Essenes. As such, Yadin maintained, the scroll was a central Torah of the sect. In it were contained elaborate instructions for building a city-size temple in Jerusalem bounded by 12 gates. Stringent codes of purity barred the lame, the diseased, and the unchaste from entering temple grounds.

Yadin's views on the origins and significance of the so-called Temple Scroll have been hotly contested. Citing doctrinal and stylistic differences between the Temple Scroll and other Essene documents, the German

Dead Sea Scrolls scholar Hartmut Stegemann has argued that the document was not an Essene manuscript but a lost book of the Old Testament—a sixth after Genesis, Exodus, Leviticus, Numbers, and Deuteronomy. The controversy is not likely to be resolved soon.

Like the Temple Scroll, the priceless scroll material residing in the Jordanian-owned Palestine Archaeological Museum became Israeli spoils of war in 1967. Even so, de Vaux and his committee of researchers were allowed to continue their work unimpeded.

The work, however, had slowed of its own accord. At first the scholars churned out translations and commentary at a laudable pace, but by 1991 they had issued only about half of the original material.

Critics have attributed the team's dilatory progress to everything from sloth to conspiracy. Decrying the delays as the "academic scandal par excellence of the 20th century," several scholars have accused the scroll committee of academic protectionism and power mongering. The researchers—who retained lifelong rights to their assigned scroll material and had the right to pass these on to protégés at their deaths—barred other academics from access to the texts. Some have imputed even darker motives to the committee. Pointing to the theological monopoly enjoyed by the mostly Catholic team, the writers Michael Baigent and Richard Leigh have proposed that the committee's laggard publication record is the result of Vatican suppression of information it has judged damaging to Christian faith.

While most scholars reject out of hand such conspiratorial theories, an increasing number have expressed outrage at the team's foot-dragging. Matters came to a head in the fall of 1991, when scholars at Hebrew Union College in Cincinnati ended the committee's decades-long control of the texts. Using a computer and a concordance—an index listing all the words and associated clauses found in the scroll material—the ac-

ademicians pieced together 16 almanacs and fragments of a document relating to the beliefs and practices of the Dead Sea sect and published them in a book. Though offering little in the way of scholarship, the gesture had an emancipating effect: In less than a month, the Huntington Library in San Marino, California, announced that its complete photographic collection of scroll material would henceforth be available to interested scholars. With grudging Israeli support, additional photographic repositories soon followed suit.

Newfound access to the long-sequestered scrolls has done little to quell controversy. The liveliest debate centers on the identity of the Qumran sect and its relationship to the scrolls. The Belgian scholars Pauline and Robert Donceel have rejected de Vaux's assertion that the community was Essene, since fragments

Constructed to resemble a lidded scroll jar, Israel's Shrine of the Book houses the seven scrolls recovered from the first cave. Inside the building, a facsimile of the Isaiah Scroll is displayed on a center platform.

of glass and other "luxury" items found on the site conflict with the sect's reported asceticism. Others, noting the congruence between Qumranian and Christian beliefs on predestination, good and evil, and material goods, have suggested that the sectarians were early Christians.

Serious scholars do not expect any doctrinal earthquakes to result from further study of the Dead Sea Scrolls. They do, however, look to these ancient parchments—older by a thousand years than the oldest previously known Hebrew manuscripts—for continuing revelations about the evolution of the Old Testament and the origins of modern Judaism and Christianity.

IN THE FOOTSTEPS OF JESUS

Just northeast of Jerusalem, in June of 1968, a routine construction project brought to light yet another telling piece of evidence from the past. As they were preparing to erect new homes in territory taken over by Israel during the Six-Day War of 1967, a crew from the Ministry of Housing unexpectedly broke through the rocky soil into several large caverns that turned out to be ancient burial chambers, part of a vast Jewish cemetery in use from the second century BC to about AD 70. As was customary, the Israel Department of Antiquities and Museums was notified, and one of its archaeologists, the Greek-born Vassilios Tzaferis, came to investigate. With a multitude of potentially rewarding sites to choose from, Tzaferis decided to concentrate on just four of the tombs. Like many others that had been found in Jerusalem, they were carved out of the limestone on which the city stands, their entrances blocked by large stone slabs. Given the number of similar burial chambers from Herod's time that had been explored, Tzaferis expected no great surprises. But among the discoveries he would make in the next weeks was one that a scholar would later describe as "an archaeological find of the first dimension."

The tomb that would cause all the excitement was typical of the period. As Tzaferis excavated the site, he came first upon a chamber about 10 feet square, with two openings that gave access to

According to tradition, Jesus took up his cross beneath this arch, where Pilate presented him to the crowd, declaring, "Ecce homo" (Behold the man). Although archaeologists determined that the arch dates from a later time, it still serves as a place of devotion and prayer.

119

another chamber dug out at a lower level. Carved into the walls of these central spaces were 12 burial niches, 9 of which held complete skeletons. The other 3 contained ossuaries—small stone boxes housing human bones. Another five ossuaries were found in the middle of the floor of the lower chamber. The tomb also yielded a great deal of pottery, including jars that had probably been filled with aromatic balsam, globular jugs for oil, and cooking pots. Touchingly, inside one of the ossuaries was a bouquet of withered flowers.

To create space in their family sepulchers for future generations, Jews customarily collected the bones of the deceased after the body had been entombed for about a year. Poorer families had to rebury the bones in pits, but the well-to-do reinterred the remains in ossuaries that were frequently decorated with inscribed patterns and sometimes with the names of the dead. The practice seems to have started in Herod's day and to have continued to the end of the second century AD. Chemical tests revealed that the eight ossuaries found by Tzaferis and his team contained the bones of 17 different people, probably representing two generations. Despite the apparent wealth of its members, the family had not been blessed by good fortune. Almost a third of the people in the chamber had died before reaching the age of 7; only 25 percent reached the age of 37; and only 2 out of the 17 lived to be more than 50. One child had apparently died of starvation, and one woman had been killed by a blow to the head.

The style of the pottery found in the tomb suggested that most of the burials had taken place in the Herodian period. One of the ossuaries also provided a dating reference. Scratched into its side in Aramaic were the words "Simon, builder of the Temple." For Jews, here was a human link with their long-lost sacred shrine; but for Christians, too, the inscription held a special significance. Textual sources made clear that the construction of Herod's Temple had commenced some time after 20 BC, and although some reports

Evidence of a long-ago crucifixion, a thick iron nail remains embedded in the heel bone of a young Jew of the first century AD. The nail's point was blunted and bent, perhaps from having hit a knot in the vertical beam of the cross into which it was driven. The grisly relic was found among other skeletal remains in a cavelike tomb just northeast of Jerusalem. A similar complex of burial chambers (above), **dating from the same period,** *includes the round stone that was rolled across the entrance to seal the tomb.*

indicated that it took only 11 years to build, others note that it was not fully completed until shortly before its destruction at the hands of the Romans in AD 70. Chances were, then, that Simon the Builder had been buried here during or shortly after the lifetime of Jesus.

But an even more potent reminder of those days came when the bones in another ossuary were sent for analysis. Although the excavators had not noticed, the young man in ossuary number 4, aged between 24 and 28, had been cruelly put to death by crucifixion.

Thousands of Jews were crucified by the Romans. Reserved for non-Roman slaves, rebels, and prisoners of war, it was the most brutal and degrading form of death they knew how to inflict. The historian Josephus wrote that the crucifixion of 3,600 Jews in AD 66 helped spark the Jewish rebellion that led to the destruction of Jerusalem four years later, when so many more people were crucified that barely enough wood for the crosses or space to erect them could be found. Yet despite the huge numbers who had perished in this way, the remains in the ossuary constituted the first authenticated physical evidence of a crucifixion in biblical times.

An inscription on the side of the ossuary revealed the victim's name: "Yehohanan, the son of Hagakol." The pathological evidence enabled scholars to construct a portrait of both the man and the manner of his dying. He was about five foot six, graceful in build, and he had suffered no traumatic injury until his crucifixion. His death, however, had been literally excruciating—a word derived from the Latin *excruciatus,* or "out of the cross." For centuries, Christian iconography has represented Jesus stretched out on the cross, secured by nails through each hand and one through his overlapping feet. But Yehohanan's legs had apparently straddled the vertical beam, each foot attached with a separate nail driven through the heel bone. And although an initial examination suggested that he had been nailed to the cross just above the wrists, more careful study refuted this conclusion; it seems more likely that, following a common practice to which Jesus was presumably an exception, Yehohanan's arms had been tied to the crossbeam. His legs had also been broken, perhaps with the intent of hastening his death by making it impossible for him to raise himself up and ease his breathing. According to the Gospel of John, this treatment was meted out to the two thieves crucified alongside Jesus. In Yehohanan's case, it was evidently a meaningless gesture: Analysis revealed he was already dead at the time.

Concerned that the coincidences of date and circumstance

might provoke speculation about the victim's identity, scholars on all sides acted to thwart any attempts to associate the find with Jesus. Avraham Biran, director of Israel's Department of Antiquities and Museums, insisted that "it was farfetched and plain silly" to suggest that this might be Jesus. Bruce Metzger, professor of New Testament at Princeton Theological Seminary, tried to avert even scholarly innuendos linking the skeleton to Jesus, because, as he pointed out, "we have absolutely no knowledge of his physical stature."

Metzger's disclaimer touched on a fundamental issue that has vexed theologians for generations. Although Jesus is one of the most influential figures the world has ever known, most of his earthly career is a blank. Apart from a few brief references in other ancient works such as Josephus, the New Testament is the only source of information on his life and mission. But the four Gospels focus more on his teachings than on biographical details and, in any event, concentrate chiefly on his last three years. Even here there are discrepancies between the various accounts, no doubt because they were probably composed some 40 to 70 years after his death and in most cases from secondhand sources at best.

For some scholars, the scarcity of hard facts about the life of Jesus poses a philosophical problem. Christianity stands squarely on the belief that Jesus was not a mythological symbol but a man of flesh and blood who lived in a particular time and place. Early Christians had no trouble reconciling this notion with the events described in Scripture: They were one and the same. "None can doubt that what is written took place," proclaimed Saint Jerome, who translated the Gospels into Latin in the fourth century. It was in this spirit of unquestioning faith that Christian pilgrims journeyed to the Holy Land to seek out relics and places associated with their Savior.

But by the 18th century, scholars inspired by the rationalism of the Enlightenment were starting to question the scriptural portrait of Jesus. Thomas Jefferson, for example, wrote a biography of Jesus that discarded many Gospel passages that he believed were not authentic. The true words, he said, were "imbedded as diamonds in dunghills." In Germany, theologians applied new critical techniques to the Scriptures in an attempt to separate the real "historical" Jesus from myth and dogma. But their efforts ultimately foundered precisely because the Gospels are a testament of faith, written not as a historical record of actual events but as a dramatic visualization proclaiming the early Church's belief in a risen Christ. And if that is the case, concluded the influential Protestant theologian Rudolf Bultmann in the 1920s, "we can now know almost nothing concerning the life and personality of Jesus."

Bultmann was undoubtedly too hasty in his judgment. He did not take into account that investigations of Jewish culture in the first century AD could be a vehicle for learning more about important influences on Jesus. Such omissions have been redressed by a new generation of scholars—Christian and Jewish, skeptics and believers—whose revived quest for historical truth has benefited from tools unavailable to earlier scriptural analysts. Scientific archaeology in particular has added greatly to knowledge of the New Testament world and, in the process, given credence to some biblical accounts. The Dead Sea Scrolls, for example, confirm that some Jews did believe in the imminent arrival of a Messiah figure, and the 1961 discovery of an inscription at Caesarea Maritima, an ancient seaport on the Mediterranean coast, proves that Pilate was indeed a first-century governor, as the Bible reports. But more dramatically than any other artifact, the crucified man found in Jerusalem sheds light on the violent world into which Jesus was born 2,000 years ago.

At the time of Jesus' birth, the Jews had been under Roman rule for about 60 years, but despite the religious liberty allowed them, they had never accepted foreign domination. While Rome's appointed overlord, Herod the Great, a Jew himself, made a gesture toward the Jews by reconstructing the Temple in Jerusalem, he seemed more intent on satisfying his own taste for splendor and pleasing his Roman masters, building palaces for his comfort and glory and erecting temples to the emperor Augustus in various cities throughout Palestine. As a consequence, his taxgatherers mercilessly squeezed an impoverished peasantry to raise funds, and resentment against Herod and the Romans festered. In Galilee, brigands and guerrillas roamed the hills; fanatical rebels called Sicarii, or daggermen, spread terror with their short knives, killing Romans and any who collaborated with them. Excavations at Qumran near the Dead Sea have revealed that the extremist Jewish

A broken limestone block, discovered by archaeologists in the ruins of a theater in Caesarea Maritima, bears the only tangible proof that Pontius Pilate ruled in Judea during the first century AD. The names "Tiberieum" and "Pilatus" in the inscription suggest that the stone was once part of a temple dedicated by Pilate to Tiberius. The block was apparently split in half years later by workmen who, scavenging it from the temple, used it to repair the theater's steps.

sect of the Essenes was preparing for the final "War between the Children of Light and the Children of Darkness." Many ordinary Jews also believed they were living through "the end of days" and awaited the coming of the Messiah—the Anointed One—a man chosen by God to free Israel from the heathen rulers whose conduct so affronted the righteous.

One Jewish tradition held that the Messiah would appear in Bethlehem, the birthplace of King David, a hill town six miles south of Jerusalem. And according to the Gospels of Matthew and Luke, that is what happened. Luke supplies most of the details of the familiar Christmas story of shepherds and angels and a baby lying in a manger, while Matthew tells of wise men from the East seeking the child "that is born King of the Jews." Word of their mission soon reached Herod, who knew immediately what he must do. His rule was difficult enough without the birth of a Messiah to stir up the populace, and he was not a man to take chances. When he failed through trickery to find the infant Jesus, he ordered the slaughter of "all the children that were in Bethlehem, and in all the coasts thereof, from two years old and under." No secular history records Herod's Massacre of the Innocents, but it was entirely in character with a man who had already put his favorite wife and two sons to death.

After the time of Jesus the Romans occupied Bethlehem, snuffing out his following and obliterating any reliable knowledge of his actual birthplace, but the tradition that he was born in a cave in the town is almost as old as Christianity itself. An early convert, Justin Martyr, who was born in Samaria in AD 100, reports being told of the cave, and when Helena, the mother of Constantine, built the first Christian Church of the Nativity about AD 325, she raised it over this spot—an event recorded by Saint Jerome, who made his home in an adjacent cave in 385 and lived in Bethlehem until his death in 420. At least one other traditional site nearby also dates to this period. In 1972, Vassilios Tzaferis discovered the well-preserved remains of a fourth-century church just east of Bethlehem, in a village called Bayt Sahur, which translates as House of the Shepherds. This shrine's earliest chapel, like the Church of the Nativity, was a natural cave and apparently commemorated the place where the angelic host announced the birth of Jesus to the shepherds.

From Bethlehem, the infant Jesus was taken to his parents'

A broad stairway leads up to the Temple Mount's south wall and to what was once a large double gate, no longer visible; the vague outline of a triple gate can be seen farther to the right. Jesus may have climbed these steps when he visited the Temple as a boy—and certainly did so later, in the week before his crucifixion.

home in Nazareth. Set high on a slope of the green Galilean hills, the town enjoyed a mild climate and a measure of peaceful isolation, but its inhabitants were not cut off from events in the wider world. The ancient caravan road between Damascus and Egypt passed only six miles away, and Roman legions used another nearby route as they marched to and from the Decapolis, a group of 10 Hellenistic cities southeast of the Sea of Galilee. The town's main disadvantage was that its water supply was restricted to one good spring, known today as Mary's Well. Indeed, Nazareth must have been a small settlement, not important enough to merit a mention in the Old Testament or in any sources outside the Bible. Such an omission led some scholars to question its existence in New Testament times at all. But in 1962, archaeologists at Caesarea Maritima found an inscription naming Nazareth as one of the towns where members of Judaism's priestly classes settled after the destruction of Jerusalem in AD 135.

Nazareth seems, then, to have been a Jewish refuge at that time, but in Jesus' day some of the more conservative elders in Jerusalem regarded Galilee as an iniquitous place, riddled with militant religious cults. Among Roman administrators, too, Galilee had a reputation as a hotbed of subversives. Sepphoris, four miles north of Nazareth, was a center of rebellion during an insurrection that followed Herod's death in 4 BC; when the Roman imperial agent Varus and his Syrian legions captured the city shortly thereafter, they took their revenge by crucifying 2,000 Jews.

Jesus thus grew up in a village close to stirring events. The Gospels, however, make virtually no mention of his youth and early manhood. In Luke, there is a brief account of a Passover visit that the 12-year-old Jesus and his family made to Jerusalem, where he ended up at the Temple, "sitting in the midst of the doctors, both hearing them, and asking them questions." Luke then jumps forward some 18 years, and he and the other Gospel writers pick up the story with Jesus' baptism. Three of the four also recount his period of fasting in the wilderness, where according to Mark he was "tempted of Satan; and was with the wild beasts; and the angels ministered unto him."

From this point, Jesus took up his mission in earnest. Matthew writes that after hearing of the arrest of John, who had baptized him, Jesus "departed into Galilee; and leaving Nazareth, he came and dwelt in Capernaum, which is upon the sea coast." Here, on the northern rim of the Sea of Galilee, near the outlet of the Jordan River, he began his teaching in Capernaum's synagogue, astounding his

listeners with the authority of his words. The people were more enraptured still when he exorcised an unclean spirit from one of their number—the first of an extraordinary succession of miraculous healings that he performed in Capernaum and throughout the area, including Jerusalem during occasional visits there.

Scholars now feel it is highly probable that the synagogue in Capernaum where he began his ministry has been found. The site was first explored by Edward Robinson in 1838 during his grand tour of the Holy Land. He realized that pieces of a building lying about the surface were from a synagogue but did not associate the location, known at the time only as Tell Hum, with Capernaum; that distinction belonged to the British army captain Charles Wilson, who conducted an excavation there on behalf of the Palestine Exploration Fund in 1866. Local inhabitants, recognizing the potential significance of the place, started rummaging about for artifacts they could sell, and builders even began making off with some of the structure's stones, threatening to obliterate what was left of it and prevent any

A broken column and other rubble lie strewn at the bottom of Jerusalem's Pool of Bethesda, said to be where Jesus healed a crippled man. Also known as the Sheep Pool, the reservoir was divided into two separate sections, one of which was used for ritual immersions, the other for washing sheep to be sacrificed at the Temple. The oldest part was cut deep into limestone rock in the second century BC. A nearby spring still flows with reddish water once believed to have curative powers.

future study. Fortunately, the entire site was purchased in 1894 by the Franciscan order, which built a high wall around it to protect against further looting.

The Franciscans allowed archaeologists to continue investigating the ruins and themselves carried out excavations in the 1920s, during which they exposed a beautiful synagogue of shining white limestone—apparently polished to resemble marble. Flights of steps led up to the platform on which the synagogue was set; an impressive row of columns graced the northern end of the nave; and there were three doorways in its facade, all facing toward Jerusalem. Father Gaudentius Orfali, who led the excavation, naturally assumed that this glorious building was the one Jesus had known.

Some 40 years later, a renewal of digging proved him wrong. Two Franciscan archaeologists from Italy, Virgilio Corbo and Stanislao Loffreda, found beneath the synagogue floor a treasure trove of more than 10,000 bronze coins from the fourth and fifth centuries AD. Although some scholars contended that these had been buried many decades after the synagogue itself was built, no one would date the structure earlier than the second century AD. However, in the course of their work, Corbo and Loffreda came upon an intriguing clue: a black basalt wall running underneath the limestone blocks. They first assumed that this was merely a foundation, but at one corner of the synagogue, the basalt wall did not align with the limestone structure above it.

Corbo and Loffreda eventually solved the puzzle by digging trenches into the synagogue floor. Nearly four feet below the limestone paving, they hit a cobbled floor of black basalt; scattered there were potsherds that could be reliably dated to the first century AD. On the basis of the similarity between the ground plan outlined by the basalt walls and the layout of other first-century synagogues discovered elsewhere—and taking into account the fact that Jews of the ancient world customarily built a new synagogue on the site of an older one—Corbo was able to declare with certainty that this was indeed the place where Jesus had taught.

Capernaum had other treasures as well. A Spanish nun named Egeria who visited the Holy Land late in the fourth century AD reported that "in Capernaum a house-church was made out of the home of the prince of the apostles, whose walls still stand today as they were." She was, of course, referring to Simon Peter, Jesus' first disciple. The Gospel of John gives Peter's original home as Bethsaida, which was itself rediscovered only in the 1980s, but Matthew mentions a house in Capernaum belonging to Peter in which Jesus frequently stayed, and Egeria's account attests to an early Christian belief in the site. During their initial excavations in the 1920s, the Franciscans found a fifth-century octagonal church some 80 feet south of the synagogue. It actually consisted of three concentric octagons, and on the floor of the innermost one were the remains of a mosaic representing a peacock, a symbol used by early Christians to represent immortality. The design of the church was significant, since it was a shape typically employed for buildings memorializing a special place or event in Christian history; the Church of the Nativity in Bethlehem was also octagonal.

Extending their investigations beyond the Capernaum synagogue, Corbo and Loffreda dug beneath the octagonal church's mosaic floor in 1968 and came upon another building, its walls scratched with the sign of the cross and with graffiti such as "Lord Jesus Christ help thy servant." The excavators believed that even this edifice was not the original: Their researches indicated that they had unearthed what was once the central room of a single-story dwelling organized around two interior courtyards. The earliest version of the structure seemed to date from the first century BC, like many other household dwellings uncovered in Capernaum; but toward the middle of the first century AD it apparently started receiving special treatment, judging from evidence of replastering and decoration of the central room and from other signs of renovation. Were early Christians already venerating the house where, according to Mark, so great a throng had once gathered to hear and be near Jesus that a hole had to be cut in the roof so that "one sick of the palsy" could be lowered on his bed to be cured by the Master? The Franciscans expressed confidence in the possibility, but the evidence connecting this house with Peter and his Lord is at best circumstantial: the description given by Egeria, inscriptions interpreted by the excavators as referring to Saint Peter but considered illegible by others, and some ancient fishhooks between layers of the floor.

The discovery of the fishhooks, though perhaps the least com-

White limestone pillars of a synagogue possibly dating to the fourth or fifth century AD overlook the walls of more ancient buildings at Capernaum, frequent scene of Jesus' early ministry. The remains of a house thought to have belonged to the disciple Peter lie beneath the octagonal structure at left.

pelling evidence for identifying the house at Capernaum, certainly called to mind the time of Jesus' Galilean ministry. Peter and his fellow disciples Andrew (his brother), James, and John were all fishermen. Indeed, boats and fishing feature prominently in Gospel stories. Jesus frequently traveled by boat to various lakeside communities and sometimes spoke from a fishing boat to crowds gathered at the water's edge. On occasion, drained by hours of preaching, with the multitude pressing so close that he "could not even eat," he and his disciples would retire to the middle of the lake. He also used a boat to keep clear of Galilee's political authorities and the increasingly hostile Pharisees—the most rigid upholders of Jewish law, who often criticized him for performing healings on the Sabbath, the prescribed day of rest. Inevitably, however, news of his deeds reached the ears of the provincial tetrarch Herod Antipas, son of Herod the Great and John the Baptist's executioner, who must have been dismayed to learn that another fiery preacher was stirring up the populace. According to Luke, "And Herod said, John have I beheaded: but who is this, of whom I hear such things? And he desired to see him."

Aware of the fate that awaited him if he fell into Herod's hands and—according to a standard Christian interpretation—believing that he had not yet completed what he intended to accomplish, Jesus took pains to avoid capture, never staying in one place for long and leaving the scenes of his miracles before soldiers could be sent against him. After his second feeding of the multitude, for example, he left right away with his disciples and sailed to Migdal, or Magdala, the home of Mary Magdalene, who had become a devoted follower after he freed her from demonic possession.

Although it was known to be just west and south of Capernaum, knowledge of the exact whereabouts of Migdal was lost early in the Christian era; parts of the site were inadvertently submerged in the 1920s when a dam raised the level of the lake. Not until the 1960s did an American underwater archaeological expedition discover the ancient harbor—a structure 300 feet long and 30 feet wide. Beginning in 1973, Franciscan monks working farther inland excavated the

Volunteer workers labor furiously to remove mud from a 2,000-year-old fishing boat found buried in the harbor of ancient Migdal, racing to keep it from being reflooded by the rising waters of the Sea of Galilee. Dug from the slime, the hull was encased in polyurethane and floated to a nearby museum. It was then submerged in a concrete tub (above, right) filled with a mixture of heated water and a synthetic wax intended to penetrate and preserve the wood.

remains of houses and uncovered a first-century AD mosaic that included a representation of a boat apparently designed to take a crew of four rowers and a helmsman.

The mosaic aroused much interest, offering a tantalizing glimpse of the kind of boat possibly used by Jesus. But 10 years later came a much more substantial find. In January 1986, after the winter rains had failed for two years running, the Sea of Galilee was at a record low level. For Yuval Lufan and his brother Moshe, members of a kibbutz not far from Migdal, the newly exposed seabed offered an opportunity to pursue their interest in archaeology. The first find was a number of ancient coins; combing the area nearby, they caught sight of the oval outline of a boat buried deep in the mud. Unsure whether they had stumbled on something significant, they asked another local amateur, who notified the Israel Department of Antiquities and Museums. Shelley Wachsmann, inspector of underwater antiquities, was dispatched forthwith to investigate. A quick examination revealed that the boat's timbers were fastened by mortise

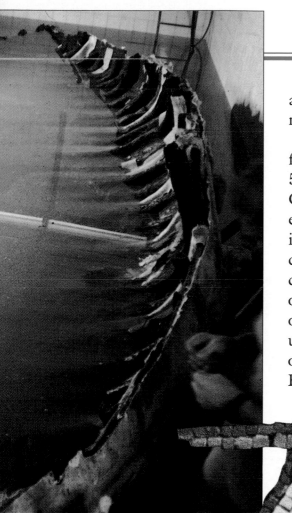

and tenon joints—a method of construction used in the Mediterranean region from the second millennium BC through Roman times.

Probing the mud in and around the boat, Wachsmann's team found a cooking pot and an oil lamp dating anywhere from about 50 BC to AD 150, suggesting that the boat might belong to the early Christian era, but more conclusive evidence would have to await a full excavation. In the meantime, for security, the boat was reburied and its location disguised with pieces of jetsam heaped up around it; decoy excavations were even begun farther down the beach. Within days, however, newspaper headlines were proclaiming the discovery of the "boat of Jesus." The reaction was startling. The Israeli Ministry of Tourism began touting the unfounded association with Jesus, and ultraorthodox Jews of nearby Tiberias responded by staging a protest on the grounds that such a relic would attract Christian missionaries. Even more worrying to the archaeologists, rumors began to circulate that the boat was a World War I Turkish bullion ship. After intruders with flashlights were seen sneaking about, the team decided to excavate the boat without further delay. An invitation to join the dig was rushed to Professor J. Richard Steffy of the Institute of Nautical Archaeology at Texas A & M University, the world's leading authority on ancient ship construction.

As the hurried preparations got under way, the rains that had held off for so long started to fall, and the team noticed that the water level was rising, threatening to cover the boat again. A desperate plea to the minister of agriculture to pump water out of the lake— which supplies most of Israel's fresh water— was turned down, but the government authority responsible for the lake did agree to build a dike around the site. Workmen arrived in the nick of time, as a strong east wind began pushing water closer and closer to the boat.

Working day and night, volunteers from local kibbutzes and

A first-century AD mosaic from a house in Migdal probably reflects the original appearance of the boat at top, found only a mile away. What appears to be a third oar in the stern was actually a sort of rudder, used by the helmsman to steer.

THE MELANCHOLY REMAINS OF A DEFIANT LAST STAND

One day in 1963, at the desolate mountaintop fortress of Masada, archaeologist Yigael Yadin stood transfixed: Before him lay the skeletons of a man, woman, and child. To Yadin, the sad remains confirmed the ancient legend of this place—a tale of heroism that ended in a suicidal act of mass defiance. "Even the veterans and the more cynical among us stood frozen," Yadin wrote, "gazing in awe at what had been uncovered; for as we gazed, we relived the final and most tragic moments of the drama."

Masada, ancient stronghold of Herod the Great, was serving as a Roman outpost when, during the First Jewish Revolt of AD 66, a fighting force of Jews known as the Sicarii overran it and held onto it. There, half a dozen years later, under the command of a firebrand named Eleazar Ben Yair, its defenders would put up such resistance that their very name—the Zealots—has come to stand for single-minded dedication.

The continued willfulness of the Zealots, however, brought a terrible price. In AD 72, the Roman governor Flavius Silva resolved to eliminate them once and for all. With his mighty 10th Legion, he laid siege to Masada. For several months the Zealots held out, but faced certain defeat once the Romans constructed a ramp giving them access to a siege tower and a battering ram, with which they began pounding the walls. At this point, the Zealots made a fateful decision.

Rather than submit to capture and suffer the humiliation of becoming slaves of the Romans, 960 men, women, and children resolved to end their lives. With grim efficiency, each Zealot warrior set to the task of slaying his own family. The survivors then cast lots to select 10 of their number who would dispatch the rest. As the Romans were about to break through the wall, hundreds of the men solemnly lay down beside the bodies of their families and offered their necks to their comrades' swords. The remaining men cast a second round of lots, this time to select one warrior to slay those who were left. The deed done, the last then took his own life.

For Yadin, easily the most poignant relics discovered here were the ostraca, or potsherds, each marked with a name. "Had we indeed found the very ostraca which had been used in the casting of the lots?" he wondered. "We shall never know for certain. But the probability is strengthened by the fact that among these 11 inscribed pieces of pottery was one bearing the name, 'Ben Yair.'"

A cave below Masada's southern wall holds the skeletons of 25 men, women, and children. "Their choice of death over slavery," wrote Yigael Yadin of Zealots like these, "elevated Masada to an undying symbol of desperate courage, a symbol which has stirred hearts throughout the last 19 centuries."

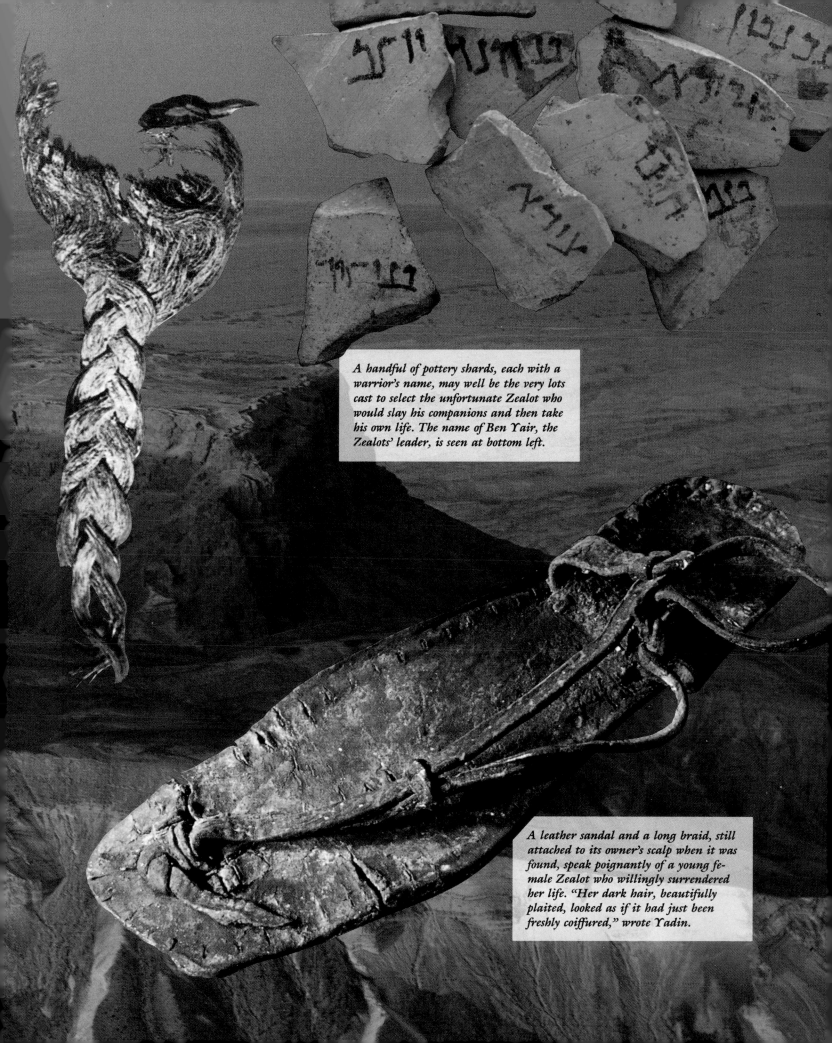

A handful of pottery shards, each with a warrior's name, may well be the very lots cast to select the unfortunate Zealot who would slay his companions and then take his own life. The name of Ben Yair, the Zealots' leader, is seen at bottom left.

A leather sandal and a long braid, still attached to its owner's scalp when it was found, speak poignantly of a young female Zealot who willingly surrendered her life. "Her dark hair, beautifully plaited, looked as if it had just been freshly coiffured," wrote Yadin.

DRAMATIC FINDS THAT GAVE LIFE TO A LEGENDARY HERO

Soon after his return from an excavation in the Judean desert in 1960, Yigael Yadin was invited to the home of the president of Israel to report on his findings. There, addressing a group that included Prime Minister David Ben-Gurion, Yadin made a startling announcement. "Your Excellency," he declared, "I am honored to be able to tell you that we have discovered 15 dispatches written or dictated by the last president of ancient Israel 1,800 years ago."

The audience was at first dumbstruck. "Then," wrote Yadin, "the silence was shattered with spontaneous cries of astonishment and joy."

The outpouring was understandable. Yadin's discovery lifted the veil of mystery that had long enshrouded one of Israel's most historic figures, the legendary ruler known as Bar-Kokhba, or "son of a star."

Like the First Jewish Revolt more than 60 years earlier, the Second Revolt—or War of Bar-Kokhba—would mark another assault against Rome. The dra-

Skulls of some of Bar-Kokhba's sup-porters, perhaps gathered up by relatives after the Roman siege, fill a basket, one of several discovered in a remote cave near the Dead Sea. "What suffering the occupants of the cave experienced in their last phase there, we can only guess," said Yadin.

ma began in AD 132, when Bar-Kokhba marshaled an army of resistance fighters to drive out the Romans. In more than three years of combat, his force seized Jerusalem and, ultimately, the whole of Judea. Viewing the reestablishment of a Jewish state as a threat to the empire, the emperor Hadrian dispatched his best legions to put down the rebellion. As a result, more than half a million Jews were slaughtered outright, and countless more perished of starvation and sickness. "Thus," reads an ancient text, "nearly the whole of Judea was made desolate."

After the defeat of Bar-Kokhba's forces at Bethar, a city seven miles southwest of Jerusalem, those who remained alive took refuge with their families and other survivors in caves scattered throughout the Judean desert. Even here, the Romans followed. Faced with surrender and enslavement, the Jews refused to yield. In time, the beleaguered starved to death.

It was here, in a three-chambered cave in a canyon overlooking the Dead Sea, that Yadin and his team found hidden within the cracks and crevices numerous items from the rebels' daily lives—powder boxes, jewelry, drinking vessels, and even door keys to the homes they hoped one day to reclaim. Close by lay baskets stacked one on top of the other, filled with skulls of some of the besieged.

Even this dramatic find would soon be overshadowed by the spectacular revelation of the letters from Bar-Kokhba himself. Secreted in a remote niche of the cave, the small bundle of writings ranks among the most significant discoveries made in the Holy Land. After 1,825 years, scholars and historians at last had decisive proof of the existence of this almost-mythical figure, and Israel had reclaimed a national hero.

Front and back views of a pair of bronze coins found at the cave site show the first name of Bar-Kokhba, "Shimeon," on the face, and the inscription "of the Freedom of Jerusalem" on the reverse. Thousands of coins like these—actually overstruck Roman pieces—were circulated during the Second Revolt.

This small bundle of crumbling papyri and wooden slats created a sensation in Israel when it proved to be a set of commands from the legendary Bar-Kokhba, ancient Israel's last president, to two of his officers. Yadin spoke of the find as not just another archaeological discovery but "the retrieval of part of the nation's lost heritage."

The pagan deities represented on these Roman-made jugs and bowls found in the cave violated the Jewish stricture against graven images. Only after the Roman images on them were defaced—such as by chipping off a nose or finger—could the vessels be considered usable.

from all over Israel completed the excavation in an astonishing eight days. As it turned out, that was the easy part. Although the vessel's timbers were remarkably well preserved, they were thoroughly waterlogged, reduced to the consistency of wet cardboard. Obviously the boat could not be lifted in such a state, and if it was allowed to dry out, it would undoubtedly disintegrate. The solution, devised by archaeologist-turned-conservator Orna Cohen of Hebrew University, was radical and untested—but it worked. First, the fragile craft was reinforced inside and out with a fiberglass frame, then enveloped in a watertight polyurethane foam cocoon. Looking, in Wachsmann's words, "like an overgrown, melted marshmallow," the package was floated out of the excavation pit, lifted onto the shore by a crane, and lowered into a water-filled conservation tank that had been specially built at the nearby kibbutz. After the delicate and tricky task of unwrapping, analysis began.

On the basis of its dimensions—about 26 feet long and 7 feet wide—Richard Steffy suggested that the boat probably had a crew of four rowers and a helmsman, just like the one portrayed in the Migdal mosaic. With a safe capacity of about a ton, it could have carried as many as 15 men weighing an average of 140 pounds. Josephus mentions a case of 10 men from Tiberias being transported across the Sea of Galilee in a single fishing boat. There are no Gospel references to the number of passengers who accompanied Jesus on his seafaring journeys, but this vessel would comfortably have accommodated most of his inner circle of 12 disciples.

There was also evidence that it had been fitted with a mast, although this—together with the stem and the sternpost—was missing. Examination of its construction showed that it had been built by a master craftsman using inferior materials, and that it had been repaired many times with timbers from older boats. Although one of the excavation team found an arrowhead at the site, in Wachsmann's opinion the vessel had not been a casualty of war. When its serviceable life had come to an end, he felt, it had simply been stripped of its usable timbers and pushed out to sink. Carbon analysis of wood samples showed that its timbers had been cut about 40 BC, give or take 80 years, or between 120 BC and AD 40.

But was it the type of boat that Jesus and his disciples had sailed in so often during those three brief years?

According to Wachsmann, it was. Styles of fishing

SOLE RELIC OF JERUSALEM'S SYNAGOGUES

In 1914, while excavating in the southeastern section of Jerusalem in what was called the City of David, a French party found a pile of building fragments at the bottom of an ancient cistern, neatly stowed by someone who had apparently hidden them there for safekeeping. Among the pieces was the limestone plaque below, dating back to the time of Herod the Great, as could be determined from its Greek inscription. "Theodotos," it proclaims, "son of Vettenos, priest and head of the synagogue."

Although there were once hundreds of synagogues in Jerusalem before Rome destroyed the Second Temple and laid the city to waste in AD 70, only this plaque

has come to light to corroborate their existence. The inscription mentions that Theodotos' father and grandfather, too, were "archisynagogus"—high synagogue officials. By counting back three generations, the archaeologists assumed that this particular synagogue had existed for at least 150 years before the fall of the holy city and had most likely been built by Theodotos' grandfather and added to by his father, as well as by Theodotos himself.

The institution of the synagogue as a place of worship probably evolved sometime after the Babylonians razed the First Temple in 586 BC. Without their Temple, the exiled Jews organized small gatherings, perhaps in private homes, to keep their faith alive through prayer and study. By Theodotos' time, these meeting houses had become centers of religious and social life—eventual models for Christian churches.

vessels changed very little in Mediterranean lands over hundreds of years, and until the beginning of the 20th century, boats of a similar size regularly plied the Sea of Galilee with seines anywhere from 500 to 1,500 feet long. This could have been the kind of net that Jesus referred to when he said that "the kingdom of heaven is like unto a net, that was cast into the sea, and gathered of every kind: Which, when it was full, they drew to shore, and sat down, and gathered the good into vessels, but cast the bad away."

But there was, of course, no evidence that Jesus had used this particular boat; the dating range even left a fair chance that it had already gone to the bottom before he was born. Nevertheless, a number of Christian visitors to the site grasped firmly at the remote possibility of a link to the Savior, begging to be allowed to touch the wood and, when that was forbidden, asking permission to touch Wachsmann's hands as the next best thing.

Although early in his ministry Jesus had avoided confronting the authorities, the time came when his mission led him to Jerusalem for the last great drama. It seemed to many a foolhardy move; even the Pharisees warned him to stay away because Herod wanted him killed. But Jesus knew what he was about. As Luke tells it, he replied to the Pharisees, "Go ye, and tell that fox, Behold, I cast out devils, and I do cures today and tomorrow, and the third day I shall be perfected." He went on to note that, according to Scripture, a prophet could not be killed except in Jerusalem.

In fact, Herod ruled not in Judea, where Jerusalem is, but in Galilee; the supreme authority in Judea was the Roman procurator, Pontius Pilate, who occupied the office from AD 26 to 36, when he was recalled in disgrace after murdering a group of Samaritans. Most of his predecessors had held the post for only three years, but the emperor Tiberius introduced longer tenures on the cynical theory that after a fly had sucked its fill on a wound, it was better to let it stay there and keep other flies away. Corruption was but one of the procurator's besetting sins, according to the Jewish philosopher Philo of Alexandria, a contemporary of Pilate's who summed up his career as a woeful catalog of "violence, robberies, ill treatment of the people, grievances, continuous executions without even the form of a trial, endless and intolerable cruelties."

Pilate's official residence was at Caesarea Maritima, but for the Passover, when Jerusalem's population doubled and emotions ran high, he moved either to Herod's palace or to the Antonia Fortress, at the northern edge of the Temple Mount, where he would be well placed to put down any disorder. At one or the other of these sites, he was soon to examine Jesus before condemning him to death. All that remains of the original Antonia Fortress is the rocky buttress on which it once stood; nor is there much trace of Herod's palace. One day in 1969, however, James Fleming, a graduate student at the American Institute of Holy Land Studies, accidentally discovered a happier place associated with Jesus' last week: the remnants of a gate in the Old City's eastern wall that may be where Jesus entered Jerusalem on Palm Sunday to the triumphant cries of his followers.

Tradition had long associated Jesus' entry with the so-called Golden Gate—whose twin arches are clearly visible in the eastern wall, though the gate itself was blocked up centuries ago. But scholars knew that it dated from Byzantine times at the very earliest. Fleming, however, was little concerned with such matters when he stopped that day to take a photograph of the gate in the morning light. Enraptured by its beauty, he was unaware that the muddy ground he was standing on—part of a Muslim cemetery—was subsiding. As he later wrote: "The heavy night rain had not yet evaporated, but I was concentrating on the view in my camera, not my sinking feet. Suddenly the earth gave way beneath me. I felt as though I was part of a rock slide. Down I went into a hole eight feet deep."

Slightly dazed, it took him a moment or two to realize that he had fallen into a pit full of human bones, apparently a mass grave. Then, as his eyes adjusted to the dim light, he saw in front of him a wall directly below the position of the Golden Gate; set into it were five wedge-shaped stones forming an arch. He scrambled out of the hole, planning to return the next day for further study, only to find when he returned that the Muslim authorities had quickly resealed the tomb into which he had fallen. Although he and other investigators got brief access to the tomb in 1972, it was soon permanently sealed. Nevertheless, Fleming's examination of the site led him to the conclusion that the arch he had seen had possibly been part of the gate through which Jesus had walked.

Not long after the glorious Palm Sunday procession, Jesus went to the Temple and, in a dramatic and calculated affront to the high priesthood, upset the tables of the moneychangers. The action amounted to a symbolic overthrow of the established religious order, which had set up the moneychangers to perform what Jewish law stated was a necessary service: trading coins bearing pagan images for money deemed acceptable by the authorities to circulate within the Temple precinct. The chief priests were incensed and sought some way to stop him without at the same time stirring up his followers. According to the Gospels, they were aided in this by Jesus' disenchanted disciple, Judas Iscariot, who offered to betray him.

The surreptitious arrest took place by night in the garden of Gethsemane, which lay just outside the city walls in the Kidron Valley. The placename has never dropped out of usage, so the site now commemorated by a church may be very close to the original location. John writes that after the arrest, Jesus was taken for interrogation first to the home of a former high priest, Annas, then to the house of the current incumbent, his son-in-law Caiaphas. At dawn he was escorted for judgment to Pilate, who alone had the power to order execution. According to all the Gospels, Pilate was reluctant to do so, repeatedly offering to free Jesus, and only condemning him to death when the crowd shouted that the procurator's clement attitude amounted to treason against Rome. This picture of a humane and scrupulous Pilate is completely at odds with the grim portrait painted in such other sources as Philo of Alexandria. It may reflect the need of first-century Christians to show the Romans—who continued to wield unassailable power—in a favorable light, but in so doing the Gospel writers heaped nearly all the blame for Jesus' judicial murder on the Jews. As for the act of crucifixion itself, there could be no denying that it was a Roman affair.

The Gospel writers relate some of the grisly events leading up to Jesus' death, but the full details of how the Romans conducted this cruelest of punishments are known from other ancient sources. The crucifixion was su-

Once open to the sky, the stone-paved courtyard where Pilate supposedly questioned Jesus is now covered by vaulting that supports a convent above. The pavement was in fact probably laid by Romans of Hadrian's time, 100 years after Jesus' death. Seen up close, the stones show traces of grooves cut to keep pedestrians and animals from slipping; they are also marked with small squares and circles incised by bored Roman soldiers who used them for various dice games.

pervised by an official known as the *carnifix serarum,* or flesh nailer; this may have been the role of the centurion who kept watch over Jesus during his agony. Once condemned, the victim was taken from the place of judgment and scourged with either a stick or a flagellum—a whip festooned with lead balls or pieces of bones. Following the beating, he was forced to shoulder the horizontal crossbeam and carry it to the execution site. John implies that Jesus carried the complete cross, but at Golgotha, which must have been a perma-

nent execution place, the uprights were probably already set in the ground. At the head of the procession marched a soldier carrying the *titulus,* an inscription written on wood that stated the defendant's name and his crime. In Jesus' case, this read, with insulting irony, "Jesus of Nazareth, the King of the Jews," written in Hebrew, Greek, and Latin.

Whether Jesus' arms were nailed to the cross as the New Testament reports, or tied with ropes as were Yehohanan's, the torment would have been extreme. Experiments conducted in the 1920s and 1930s showed that death would have occurred in a matter of hours as a result of asphyxiation, with the muscles of the chest and diaphragm progressively weakening until breathing became impossible. To prolong the agony, Roman executioners devised a kind of seat to support the body and make it easier to breathe. Josephus mentions a case of three Jews who survived on the cross for three days.

For Jesus, presumably weak from the terrible scourging by Pilate's soldiers, release was mercifully fast—in about six hours. Pilate himself seems to have been surprised that the end came so soon, asking a centurion for confirmation before giving permission for the body to be delivered into the care of Joseph of Arimathea, a wealthy

Highly speculative theories of the 19th century posited this rocky escarpment—its dark holes eerily suggesting a skull's empty eye sockets—as Golgotha, the site of Jesus' crucifixion. Numerous tombs have been found nearby, but all date to the 7th and 8th centuries BC and show no signs of having been used in Jesus' time.

follower of Jesus. With the help of Mary, the mother of James the Less, and Mary Magdalene, Joseph laid the body in a new, rock-hewn tomb, then rolled a stone against its entrance. John says this was in a garden near the place where he had been crucified.

The traditional site of the tomb—the scene of Jesus' triumphant resurrection, the very bedrock of the Christian faith—was desecrated in AD 135 by the Roman emperor Hadrian, who built a shrine to Venus over it. The first reference to the spot after the New Testament's was made in AD 160 by a Christian who had just visited Jerusalem. He claimed that the tomb was in the middle of the city, although the Scriptures said that Jesus was killed outside the city gate, and Jewish burials never took place inside the city walls. There was, however, no contradiction, because a new wall was built in AD 44, encompassing many parts of the city that had previously lain outside the walls in Jesus' time. Furthermore, despite official efforts at suppression, early Christians living in the area surely venerated the place, and likely passed on their knowledge to later generations. Thus when Constantine's mother, the empress Helena, made her pilgrimage early in the fourth century, she might very well have picked up accurate information and built the Church of the Holy Sepulcher just where it belonged.

Two domes crown the huge, sprawling Church of the Holy Sepulcher, believed by many scholars to mark the actual sites of Golgotha and Jesus' tomb. The present building was begun by 12th-century Crusaders, but older versions trace back to the 4th century AD. Now within Jerusalem's crowded Old City, the site was in Jesus' time outside the city walls, where executions and burials would have taken place. Archaeological evidence that the area was once a garden and the discovery there of a cemetery dating to no earlier than the 1st century BC match New Testament accounts that Jesus was laid to rest in a new tomb in a garden.

Mute evidence of Jewish tragedy and Roman violence, the remarkably well preserved bones of a young woman's forearm and hand (opposite) *lean against the blackened stone of a house put to the torch in AD 70, when legionaries systematically looted and burned Jerusalem while crushing a Jewish revolt. The bones were discovered in the small kitchen room at bottom center of the photograph above, part of what archaeologist Nahman Avigad dubbed the Burnt House for the extraordinary amounts of ash and soot found among the ruins.*

Despite the tradition that Helena's basilica and other churches built on top of it mark the authentic site of the tomb, an alternative was proposed in 1842 by a German pastor, Otto Thenius, who favored a hill 150 yards north of the present walled city because of two caves that gave it a skull-like appearance. The notion became popular with Protestants and was adopted by General Charles Gordon, the great British war hero who would die attempting to defend Khartoum against a Mahdist onslaught. Gordon had always had a love for things mystic, and in 1883 he set out to find the garden tomb mentioned by John, with little thought of applying any kind of scientific or historical analysis to the task. Using a bizarre method of divination, he laid a drawing of Jesus' skeleton on a map of ancient Jerusalem so that the cranium lay on the area identified by Thenius as Golgotha, the Place of the Skull. Without further ado, a tomb nearby was selected as the holy spot. Despite compelling evidence to the contrary, it continues to attract many pilgrims.

As far as the faithful are concerned, of course, the precise location is of little religious significance. After all, the central tenet of Christianity is embodied in the words of the two men "in shining garments" who, according to Luke, were found by Jesus' grieving followers at the tomb on Easter morning: "Why seek ye the living among the dead? He is not here, but is risen."

Christianity itself would spring to life in the wake of these events, quickly spreading along the same roads that had brought Rome's conquering armies to Palestine. For the Jews, however, the suffering at the hands of those armies went from bad to worse, as two major revolts in the next hundred years were brutally suppressed. (The Christian community in Jerusalem was also wiped out in the crackdown.) Their holiest shrine obliterated, their access to Jerusalem denied, the Jews began an enforced diaspora that by all rights should have doomed their culture to oblivion. But by nurturing their faith and their traditions wherever they found themselves, they managed to keep their ways alive. And more than 18 centuries after it had apparently disappeared for good, Israel returned as a nation on the very land where its people's roots ran so deep.

HEROD: THE MASTER BUILDER

Rising more than 1,300 feet above the western shore of the Dead Sea, the lofty palace-fortress known as Masada has stood for more than 2,000 years as a powerful symbol of one of history's most controversial rulers, Herod the Great, the half-Arab, half-Edomite Jewish king of Judea. One of the most innovative builders of the ancient world, this mighty monarch distinguished his reign not only with the resurrection of the Temple at Jerusalem but also with the construction of a series of dazzling palaces, as well as an entire city and harbor, remarkable for their lavish scale and the engineering prowess they reveal.

King Herod reached the height of his power in 37 BC, having snatched the throne of Judea from the ruling Maccabean dynasty with the blessing of the Roman leaders Mark Antony and Augustus Caesar. Notorious for his despotic nature and overriding ambition, Herod would spend the bulk of his 33-year reign paying tribute to his Roman benefactors while simultaneously attempting to curry favor with his Judean subjects. As a result, the king's reign was characterized by contradiction. He could be extraordinarily ruthless, once ordering the execution of three of his own sons; but he also adhered to Jewish customs and laws, abstaining, for example, from pork. "I would rather be Herod's pig," said Augustus Caesar, "than his son."

In 36 BC, Herod began transforming the lonely rock of Masada into a magnificent palace-fortress. The bold design, incorporating elements of the then-popular Hellenistic style, took advantage of the inaccessible location to provide a refuge if the Judean uprising Herod feared should ever occur. A high casemate wall dotted with guard towers encircled the whole of Masada's high plateau. Inside lay a bustling complex, complete with a sumptuous palace, several smaller royal residences, a number of storerooms and administrative buildings, a synagogue, and even a public bathhouse. Here, the king could entertain himself and his guests in splendid isolation.

Ironically, the final fate of Masada would prove quite different from anything Herod could have envisioned. At the beginning of the Great Revolt of AD 66, 70 years after his death, when the band of Jewish rebels known as the Sicarii overran Masada, his fortifications enabled the defenders to withstand four or five months of siege by Roman forces.

Today, the story of Herod's Masada and the ancient Jews' heroic stand there has found new life, thanks in large measure to the Israeli archaeologist Yigael Yadin. Working with an army of colleagues and volunteers, Yadin began extensive excavations in 1963. They found conditions at the remote, sun-seared location difficult, but for Yadin and his fellow countrymen, the dig would be far more than a purely historical endeavor. "Masada has become for us a symbol," he explained. "The poet's words 'Masada will not fall again' have become a rallying cry for the younger generation and, indeed, for the whole nation."

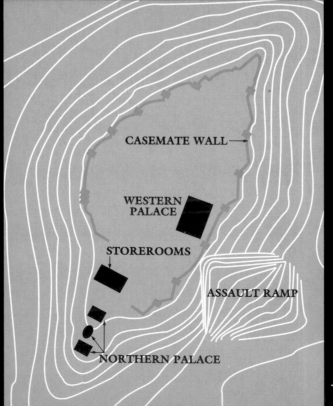

CASEMATE WALL —→

WESTERN PALACE

STOREROOMS

ASSAULT RAMP

NORTHERN PALACE

A topographical map of Masada shows the locations of two of Herod's palaces, along with storerooms and the casemate wall around the edge of the plateau. Abutting the wall is the assault ramp constructed by Roman forces in AD 73.

Seen today against the backdrop of the Dead Sea, Masada remains an imposing sight. In the foreground, the remains of Herod's 2,000-year-old northern palace cling to the face of the mountain.

Covered with debris for more than 2,000 years, these wall paintings discovered in Herod's northern palace endured thanks to the dry climate. Along with other elaborate frescoes that imitated the popular Hellenistic trompe l'oeil style, they were intended to give the plaster walls the appearance of stone and marble.

Hewn from solid rock, this underground cistern held a little more than a million gallons of water. Supplying water to the aerie required ingenuity; Herod's engineers devised a system of dams and aqueducts to take advantage of periodic flash floods

The ruins of a Roman-style bath-house, complete with separate chambers for cold, warm, and hot ablutions, were discovered on the mountain's northern summit. The pillars supported a floor, creating a shallow area filled with superheated air for sweat baths.

Capping the mountaintop complex at Masada, King Herod's northern palace was a marvel of ancient engineering. Boldly original in design, the palace descended the mountain's northern scarp in three separate terraces resembling a giant staircase, the lowest level perched at the edge of a dizzying precipice. The finished structure was so well integrated into the face of the mountain that it was largely overlooked by archaeologists until 1950.

The construction of this three-tiered palace pressed the skill of Herod's builders to the absolute limits, especially while working on the narrow and dangerous lower level. "In order to erect anything at all on it," wrote archaeologist Yigael Yadin, "Herod's engineers had to fashion some kind of artificial platform with the aid of powerful supporting walls, up to 80 feet in height, hanging over the abyss."

The edifice was unlike anything in the ancient world. Sheltered from the searing desert winds, Herod's hanging palace afforded him an unprecedented degree of luxury. On the uppermost terrace a semicircular colonnade enclosed the king's royal apartments. A rounded building on the middle terrace, 60 feet below, is thought to have been used for dining and other entertainments. The lower edge, 45 feet farther down the mountain, featured an open court ringed with a columned portico.

The degree of luxury available in such an unlikely place is astounding to modern scholars. Only a man so single-minded and all-powerful as Herod could have accomplished the impossible.

Not content with his accomplishments at Masada, Herod resolved sometime around 23 BC to construct an even more formidable palace-fortress eight miles south of Jerusalem. There, at a site to called Herodium, the king's engineers tackled an enormous hill, reshaping it in the process.

The main feature of this exotic new palace was a cylindrical outer wall. Approximately 200 feet in diameter, the completed enclosure rose 90 feet above the bedrock on which it stood. To increase its strength, Herod's builders gave the structure a double wall, filling the space in between with seven stories of rooms and storage areas and a winding corridor 11½ feet wide. In addition, they encased the lower part of the fortress in tons of earth and rock, creating an artificial mountain in the Judean desert with slopes ranging up to 60 feet in height.

The new stronghold offered Herod a virtually impenetrable defense. His mighty tower could be entered only by means of a steep stairway almost 500 feet long that climbed the outside of the fortress for some 300 feet, then ran through the massive pile for another 200 feet. But Herod saw to his comfort even here. Inside the rounded structure he built a spacious private palace in the elegant Hellenistic style he favored. A large sunken courtyard dominated the eastern half, while the western half contained the king's living and sleeping quarters as well as a triclinium, which was an official reception room and dining area.

Perhaps the most remarkable feature of Herodium was the four prominent towers that guarded the outer wall, one at each point of the compass. Three of these, each containing about 20 rooms, came up only as high as the retaining wall itself. A fourth, on the eastern point, was apparently solid for 60 feet, then rose 70 or so feet above the wall's rim. It contained a second royal apartment. Blocked off by the outer wall, the chambers of the main dwelling were doubtless hot and airy, but those atop the eastern tower afforded both a breeze and a spectacular view of the desert.

All this was not enough to satisfy Herod. Although the protected fortress was largely self-sufficient, with cisterns to hold and accumulate water, the king built an even larger complex of support structures at the base of his mountain. And he added another palace as well, complete with formal gardens and a gallery overlooking a 1,100-foot-long terrace that may have been used to race horses for show. Another lavish feature of this palace complex was a luxurious bathing pool measuring nearly 30,000 square feet. Fed by an aqueduct running from springs three and a half miles away, it allowed members of the royal family to while away the hours in small boats or in the colonnaded pavilion at its center. In all, the massive complex at Herodium covered 45 acres, making it the third-largest palace in the entire Roman Empire. By the time of its completion, King Herod had firmly established himself as a major power in the ancient world.

POOL

PAVILION

FORMAL
GARDEN

LOWER PALACE

MAIN
STAIRWAY

TERRACE

A plan of Herodium reveals the scope of Herod's vision; the fortress-palace atop the height is dwarfed by the enormous lower palace, terrace, and pool.

In a bird's-eye view, the structures of Herodium are plainly visible. Seen against a backdrop of Arab towns, the man-made mountain still dominates the scene as it did in Herod's time.

ot only did Herod lend his name to the majestic palace-fortress, but, according to ancient texts, Herodium was also the site of his burial. "The bier was of solid gold, studded with precious stones," wrote the first-century AD historian Flavius Josephus, describing Herod's funeral ceremonies in the year 4 BC, "and had a covering of purple, embroidered with various colors; on this lay the body enveloped in a purple robe, a diadem encircling the head and surmounted by a crown of gold, the scepter beside his right hand."

Josephus goes on to describe a grand procession joined by hundreds of the king's subjects, but his description of the final resting place remains vague. To date, the exact location of Herod's remains has eluded modern archaeologists; and in fact, it is only to be expected that the author of so many nearly superhuman accomplishments should seem to be able to exercise his will beyond the grave. In life, Herod created his citadel to shield him from usurpers; in death, it appears, the mountain fortress and its associated structures continue to protect their invincible master.

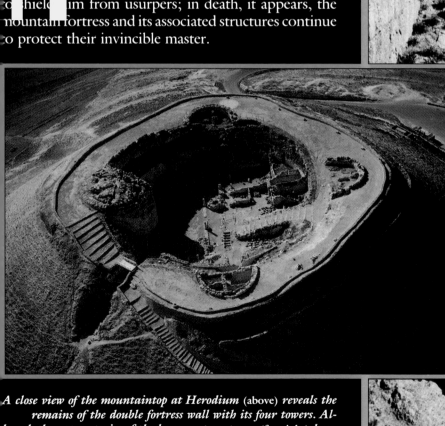

A close view of the mountaintop at Herodium (above) *reveals the remains of the double fortress wall with its four towers. Although the upper stories of the large eastern tower* (far right) *have long since collapsed, the solid base appears strong enough to have supported the lofty royal apartment described in ancient texts.*

For all of his stupendous achievements at Herodium and Masada, Herod did not rest. His kingdom, he realized, had desperate need of trading facilities, but no natural harbor that would have been suited to the construction of a seaport. Herod resolved the dilemma with typical bravado. Though such a thing had never before been accomplished, the master builder undertook to erect a vast harbor complex. It was, to say the least, an astonishing and audacious feat of engineering skill.

Along the coast Herod discovered a city that was in decline, wrote Flavius Josephus, "whose location was well suited to receive his generosity. This he rebuilt entirely in marble and ornamented with a most splendid palace." The site Herod selected, roughly 30 miles north of the area occupied by the present-day city of Tel Aviv, was a Phoenician trading post that had long ago fallen into ruin. Herod's engineers and builders began work in the year 22 BC, determined to transform a dangerous and inhospitable stretch of Mediterranean coastline into a major port.

Thousands of workmen were set to the task of constructing massive artificial breakwaters, employing the most advanced techniques available. Teams of divers floated hollow wooden forms into position over manmade rubble foundations, then sank them with stone, mortar, and chains. A special marine concrete, recently devised by Roman engineers, was poured underwater through wooden tubes with flexible leather joints. The addition of volcanic ash enabled the mixture to harden.

As the concrete blocks solidified, boulders were piled against the sides to prevent them from washing away. By repeating this process over and over again, Herod's work force eventually created a pair of massive breakwaters that reached out half a mile from shore to enclose a protected anchorage. Next, the breakwaters were paved with cut stone and fitted with docks, warehouses, and a monumental lighthouse that could be seen far out at sea. Six colossal bronze statues stood guard over the entrance to the harbor.

Herod gave his revitalized city the name of Caesarea, a tribute to his patron, the Roman emperor Augustus Caesar (today it is referred to as Caesarea Maritima). "We don't have a list of engineering wonders of the ancient world," declares Robert Hohlfelder, professor of history at the University of Colorado, "but if we did, Caesarea Maritima would be ranked in the top five."

The remnants of the once-thriving seaport of 100,000 inhabitants present a unique challenge to archaeologists. "Of all the great seaports of antiquity," says Dr. Hohlfelder, "Caesarea Maritima is the only one that is readily accessible to underwater archaeologists." Instead of trowels and brushes, however, archaeologists working in the ancient harbor must use diving gear as they hunt among the submerged ruins, battling frigid waters and powerful currents to explore the 2,000-year-old breakwaters.

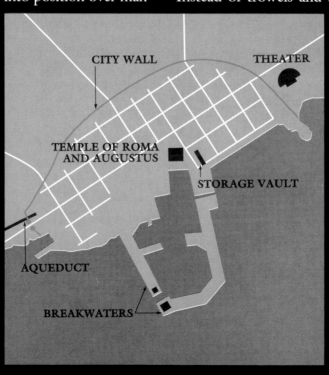

CITY WALL

THEATER

TEMPLE OF ROMA AND AUGUSTUS

STORAGE VAULT

AQUEDUCT

BREAKWATERS

Herod's harbor complex, which took just over 10 years to build, featured a pair of concrete breakwaters, storage facilities, an oil-burning lighthouse, and a sluice system that periodically flushed the harbor to prevent silting. "Thus," wrote Josephus, "by lavish expenditure, the king conquered nature herself."

Though partially covered with silt and coral, the submerged remains of the once-mighty harbor—including its breakwaters—are still visible today.

Grain, wine, and other goods unloaded from ships in the harbor were stored in stone vaults like this one. Because of the enormous volume of material that passed through Caesarea, at least 100 vaults were built near the harbor and along the break-waters. Some were as much as 100 feet long.

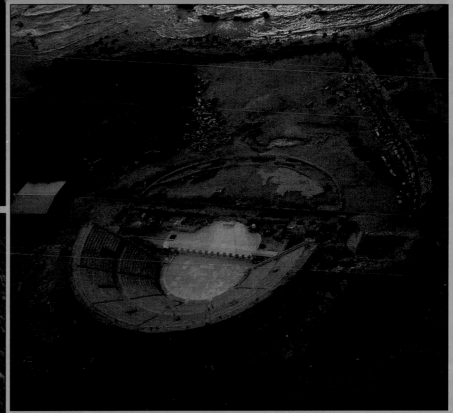

The stone benches of the theater at Caesarea Maritima could accommodate about 4,000 people. Serving in King Herod's time for performances of Greek and Roman plays, it has been restored and is used today by the Israel Philharmonic and other world-famous orchestras for summer concerts.

aesarea was a city to be proud of. Josephus tells us that here, "as nowhere else," the master builder "displayed the innate grandeur of his character." Tons of fine white marble and statuary were imported to bring Herod's "magnificent plan" to life.

Herod laid out his city according to the established Roman grid plan, with a palace and government buildings enclosed within a high defensive wall, outside of which were constructed an amphitheater and a theater. Although the remote location presented a challenge to the king's engineers, the city nonetheless boasted sea-flushed sewers and an aqueduct to bring fresh water from the springs of Mount Carmel, five miles distant.

Caesarea would remain a major seaport and cultural center for six centuries, a worthy tribute to the builder-king. In time the dazzling harbor, built on an unsuspected geological fault, would fall into ruin, but its reputation would endure. "This," declared one awe-struck visitor to the site, "is Herod's immortality."

The city's many baths and fountains required an enormous supply of fresh water, which was carried by this high-level aqueduct. A portion of Herod's original aqueduct can be seen in the right foreground; two centuries later the emperor Hadrian added a second one, building along the western side of King Herod's.

HISTORY WRITTEN IN SCRIPTURE AND IN STONE

CANAANITE CULTURES
3000-1200 BC

GOLDEN CALF

PERIOD OF JUDGES/
UNITED MONARCHY
1200-920 BC

POMEGRANATE

DIVIDED MONARCHY
920-586 BC

CAPTIVES LEAVING LACHISH

The Land of Canaan—known later in ancient history as Israel and later still, under the Romans, as Palestine—was dotted with walled towns and crisscrossed by trade routes as early as 3000 BC. Biblical tradition names Canaan as the place where a people who would become the Israelites passed generations in nomadic wanderings, led by patriarchs beginning with Abraham. Some scholars say they settled in Egypt and flourished under the Hyksos, a conquering Asiatic people, possibly from Canaan, who were eventually overthrown by the Egyptians. Exodus recounts the subsequent enslavement of the Hebrews, their deliverance from bondage by Moses, and their return to the wilderness south of Canaan.

By 1200 BC, although Egypt remained the region's dominant power, the early Canaanite city-states still maintained their independence. Their religion included the worship of El, whose symbol was the bull, of which skilled artisans produced images like the Golden Calf above, a gilded bronze. Made in the second millennium BC in the city of Byblos, the figure was buried as a gesture of devotion in the foundation of a sanctuary.

At the dawning of the Iron Age, around 1200 BC, the Israelites were settling down in the uplands of Canaan, while the Philistines and other so-called Sea Peoples secured the coastal lowlands. In this turbulent time, many old walled towns were destroyed or changed hands after a struggle. Villages in the hill country were ringed by cultivated terraces, and the inhabitants used new iron tools to carve cisterns out of living rock for trapping and storing water. According to the Bible, the Israelites lived in a loose coalition of 12 tribes, with nonhereditary leaders called judges serving as sages and generals. But fear of the Philistines eventually led the tribes to unite under a monarch.

The United Monarchy, flourishing from about 1030 to 920 BC under Saul, David, and Solomon, coexisted with other small kingdoms in the area, fought the Philistines, and traded with the Phoenicians. Israel was soon able to launch massive building projects, most notably in Jerusalem, where Solomon erected a magnificent temple. The decorative ivory pomegranate above, dating from the eighth century BC, is its only known relic.

With Solomon's death in 920 BC, Israel's golden age ended. Solomon's grand public works had burdened his people with heavy taxation and forced labor. The northern region rejected his son Rehoboam as king, and the United Monarchy split into two feuding realms: Israel in the north and Judah in the south.

Divided, the once-great nation was conquered two centuries later from the north by Assyria. Israel's capital, Samaria, fell first, in 722; rolling southward, the Assyrian king Sennacherib took one of Judah's main cities, Lachish, in 701, and marched thousands of survivors into exile in Assyria. To commemorate his triumph, he commissioned the relief above, which shows the subjugation of Israelite captives.

After trying and failing to take Judah's capital, Jerusalem, the Assyrians declined as a power; in 612, their own capital, Nineveh, fell to the Babylonians. Babylon went on to a punishing victory over Egypt, and in 588 the Babylonian king Nebuchadnezzar began a lengthy effort to seize Jerusalem. In 586 his army finally breached the defenses, destroying the city and Solomon's Temple, and ending Judah's independence.

One of the earliest sites of human habitation, cradle of three great faiths, the region known as the Holy Land is a surprisingly small, rugged stretch of the Near East with a long and eventful history. Among its most compelling periods is the time from the emergence of the Israelites in Canaan near the end of the 13th century BC to the first decades of the Christian era, a period for which the Bible has long served as the chief source of information. In recent years, archaeological discoveries have brought new perspectives to light on this and more distant phases of the region's past. The brief summaries on these pages reflect both the rich biblical legacy and what has been learned from the archaeological record.

EXILE AND RETURN
586-323 BC

EARRING

GREEK AND EARLY
ROMAN PERIOD
323-4 BC

TEMPLE COIN

EARLY ROMAN AND
CHRISTIAN PERIOD
4 BC-AD 135

STONE TABLET

The victorious Nebuchadnezzar executed many of Judah's leaders and sent the king and 10,000 survivors into exile in Babylonia. After Nebuchadnezzar's death in 562 BC, the Babylonian Empire declined, falling in 539 to Cyrus, king of Persia.

Cyrus administered the former Assyrian and Babylonian territories in peace, strengthening local governments and urging displaced peoples to return home. Although the Persians had major effects on the administration, economy, roads, and communications of the former Israelite kingdoms, their influence is unapparent in surviving everyday artifacts; such Persian-style items as the gold calf's-head earring above were reserved for members of the Persian elite.

The Persians oversaw a reconstruction of the Temple at Jerusalem, completed in 516; under the Jewish governor Nehemiah, the community reaffirmed its ancient social and religious principles. The territory changed masters again beginning in 333 BC, when Alexander the Great launched his assault on Persian hegemony. By the time of his death 10 years later, he had added their domains of Syria, Egypt, and Judah (also known as Judea) to his empire.

Upon Alexander's death, Ptolemy, one of his four generals, seized Judea and made it an Egyptian province. Syria took over in 198 BC when Ptolemy's heirs lost out to the Seleucids—descendants of another of Alexander's generals. In 167, the Syrian king Antiochus IV banned Judaism in Jerusalem in favor of Greek gods; led by Judah Maccabee, the Jews revolted and recaptured the Temple. In 142 they won independence from Syria, and with it the right to religious self-determination.

Now under Jewish rule for the first time since its fall to Babylon in 586, the state grew in size and power. But toward the middle of the first century BC, squabbles in the ruling Hasmonean family brought down the dynasty and gave Rome a foothold in the region.

Occupied in 63 BC by the Roman general Pompey, Judea later became a client state, with much-reduced boundaries. Herod the Great, made king of Judea by the Roman Senate in 40 BC, ruled the territory with an iron hand until his death in 4 BC. His monumental building projects included the reconstruction of Jerusalem's Temple, the facade of which is shown on the coin above, struck in AD 135.

Herod's death left Judea an impoverished, rebellious kingdom, which by AD 6 was put under the rule of Roman procurators, or caretakers. The procurator from AD 26 to 36 was Pontius Pilate, named on the stone tablet above from Caesarea Maritima as a first-century governor. His dates place him in Judea at the time of Jesus' crucifixion, traditionally set at AD 30.

The new religion that grew up around Jesus was at first centered in Jerusalem, where the faithful lived communally and continued to worship at the Temple. Later, the journeys of Paul and other missionaries spread Christianity among non-Jewish peoples. Meanwhile, the corruption and cruelty of a succession of Roman procurators bred growing unrest in Judea, leading in AD 66 to the First Jewish Revolt. Quashing the rebellion, the Romans destroyed Jerusalem and the Temple in AD 70. The survivors made their last stand at Masada in AD 73, preferring mass suicide to life under Roman rule. In one further uprising, Jewish rebels took Jerusalem in 132 and held it until 135, when superior Roman forces finally wiped them out. Jews were banned from the city, and the Jewish-Christian community was dispersed.

ACKNOWLEDGMENTS

The editors are grateful to Hershel Shanks, editor of Biblical Archaeology Review, *and his staff for their invaluable assistance in the preparation of this volume. The editors also wish to thank the following individuals and institutions:*

Joshua Brilliant, Tel Aviv University, Tel Aviv; Robert J. Bull, Drew University, Madison, New Jersey; Peter Clayton, Hemel Hempstead, Herts; Jon A. Cole, Walla Walla University, College Place, Washington; Peter Dorrell, Institute of Archeology, London; Steven Feldman, Biblical Archaeology Society, Washington, D.C.; Shimon Gibson, Palestine Exploration Fund, London; Robert L. Hohlfelder, University of Colorado, Colorado Springs; Amos Kloner, Director, Israel Antiquities Authority, Jerusalem; Irene Lewitt, Israel Museum, Jerusalem; Cheryl R. W. McGowan, Biblical Archaeology Society, Washington, D.C.; Stephen Sachs, University of Maryland, College Park; Lawrence E. Stager, Harvard University, Cambridge, Massachusetts; Jonathan Tubb, Department of Western Asiatics, British Museum, London; James C. VanderKam, University of Notre Dame, Notre Dame, Indiana; Lital Yadin, Jerusalem; Joseph Yellin, Hebrew University, Jerusalem.

PICTURE CREDITS

BIBLIOGRAPHY

BOOKS

Albright, William Foxwell. *The Archaeology of Palestine and the Bible*. New York: Fleming H. Revell, 1932/33.

Aldred, Cyril. *Akhenaten*. London: Thames and Hudson, 1988.

Allegro, John. *The Dead Sea Scrolls*. Baltimore: Penguin Books, 1966.

Archaeological Institute of America (Comp.). *Archaeological Discoveries in the Holy Land*. New York: Bonanza Books, 1967.

Avigad, Nahman. *Discovering Jerusalem*. Nashville: Thomas Nelson Publishers, 1983.

Avi-Yonah, Michael. *The Holy Land*. New York: Holt, Rinehart and Winston, 1972.

Avi-Yonah, Michael (Ed.). *Encyclopedia of Archaeological Excavations in the Holy Land* (Vol. 1). Englewood Cliffs, N.J.: Prentice-

Hall, 1975.

Avi-Yonah, Michael, and Ephraim Stern (Eds.). *Encyclopedia of Archaeological Excavations in the Holy Land* (Vol. 3). Englewood Cliffs, N.J.: Prentice-Hall, 1977.

Baigent, Michael, and Richard Leigh. *The Dead Sea Scrolls Deception*. New York: Summit Books, 1991.

Barkay, Gabriel. *Ketef Hinnom: A Treasure Facing Jerusalem's Walls*. Jerusalem: Israel Museum, 1986.

Ben-Gurion, David (Ed.). *The Jews in Their Land*. London: Aldus Books, 1966.

Campbell, Edward F., Jr., and David Noel Freedman (Eds.). *The Biblical Archaeologist Reader* (Vol. 3). Garden City, N.Y.: Anchor Books, 1970.

Corcos, Georgette (Ed.). *The Glory of the Old Testament*. New York:

Villard Books, 1984.

Cornfeld, Gaalyah, and David Noel Freedman. *Archaeology of the Bible: Book by Book*. San Francisco: Harper & Row, 1976.

Dever, William G. *Recent Archaeological Discoveries and Biblical Research*. Seattle: University of Washington Press, 1990.

Drower, Margaret S. *Flinders Petrie*. London: Victor Gollancz, 1985.

Eban, Abba. *Heritage*. New York: Summit Books, 1984.

Encyclopaedia Judaica. Jerusalem: Keter Publishing House, 1973.

Eydoux, Henri-Paul. *The Story of Archaeology*. New York: World Publishing, 1971.

Finkelstein, Israel. *The Archaeology of the Israelite Settlement*. Jerusalem: Israel Exploration Society, 1988.

Fox, Robin Lane. *The Unauthorized Version*. New York: Viking, 1991.

Hindson, Edward E. *The Philistines and the Old Testament.* Grand Rapids: Baker Book House, 1986.

Holum, Kenneth G., and Robert L. Hohlfelder (Eds.). *King Herod's Dream: Caesarea on the Sea.* New York: W. W. Norton, 1988.

Illustrated Dictionary and Concordance of the Bible. New York: Macmillan, 1986.

The Israelites (Emergence of Man series). New York: Time-Life Books, 1975.

Josephus, Flavius. *The Jewish War.* Translated by G. A. Williamson, revised by E. Mary Smallwood. London: Penguin Books, 1988.

Kenyon, Kathleen M.:
The Bible and Recent Archaeology (rev. ed.). Atlanta: John Knox Press, 1987.
Digging Up Jericho. New York: Frederick A. Praeger, 1957.

King, Philip J. *American Archaeology in the Mideast.* Philadelphia: American Schools of Oriental Research, 1983.

Kollek, Teddy, and Moshe Pearlman. *Jerusalem.* Jerusalem: Steimatzky, 1983.

Kraeling, Carl H. *The Synagogue* (Excavations at Dura-Europos series). New Haven: Yale University Press, 1979.

Mazar, Amihai. *Archaeology of the Land of the Bible* (Anchor Bible Reference Library). New York: Doubleday, 1990.

Millard, Alan. *Treasures from Bible Times.* Tring, U.K.: Lion Publishing, 1985.

Miller, J. Maxwell, and John H. Hayes. *A History of Ancient Israel and Judah.* Philadelphia: Westminster Press, 1986.

National Geographic Society. *Everyday Life in Bible Times* (The Story of Man Library). Washington, D.C.: National Geographic Society, 1967.

Negev, Avraham (Ed.). *The Archaeological Encyclopedia of the Holy Land* (3d ed.). New York: Prentice Hall Press, 1990.

Parkes, P. A. *Current Scientific Techniques in Archaeology.* London: Croom Helm, 1986.

Pearlman, Moshe. *Digging Up the Bible.* New York: William Morrow, 1980.

Perez, Nissan N. *Focust East.* New York: Harry N. Abrams, 1988.

Pritchard, James B. (Ed.). *The Harper Atlas of the Bible.* New York: Harper & Row, 1987.

Rasmussen, Carl G. *Zondervan NIV Atlas of the Bible.* Grand Rapids: Zondervan Publishing House, 1989.

Renfrew, Colin, and Paul Bahn. *Archaeology.* New York: Thames and Hudson, 1991.

Roberts, David:
The Holy Land. London: Studio Editions, 1989.
Yesterday the Holy Land. Grand Rapids: Zondervan Publishing House, 1982.

Robinson, Edward. *Biblical Researches in Palestine.* New York: Arno Press, 1977.

Rogerson, John. *Atlas of the Bible.* New York: Facts On File, 1985.

Schiffer, Michael B. (Ed.). *Archaeological Method and Theory* (Vol. 1). Tucson: University of Arizona Press, 1989.

Shanks, Hershel. *The City of David.* Washington, D.C.: Biblical Archaeology Society, 1975.

Shanks, Hershel (Ed.):
Ancient Israel: A Short History from Abraham to the Roman Destruction of the Temple. Washington, D.C.: Biblical Archaeology Society, 1988.

Shanks, Hershel, and Dan P. Cole (Eds.):
Archaeology in the World of Herod, Jesus, and Paul (Vol. 2 of *Archaeology and the Bible: The Best of BAR*). Washington, D.C.: Biblical Archaeology Society, 1990.
Early Israel (Vol. 1 of *Archaeology and the Bible: The Best of BAR*. Washington, D.C.: Biblical Archaeology Society, 1990.

Silberman, Neil Asher. *Digging for God and Country.* New York: Alfred A. Knopf, 1982.

Simmons, James C. *Passionate Pilgrims.* New York: William Morrow, 1987.

Smith, George Adam. *The Historical Geography of the Holy Land* (25th ed.). New York: Harper and Brothers, n.d.

Sumption, Jonathan. *Pilgrimage.*

London: Faber & Faber, 1975.

Swinglehurst, Edmund. *The Romantic Journey.* London: Pica Editions, 1974.

Tubb, Jonathan N., and Rupert L. Chapman. *Archaeology and the Bible.* London: British Museum Publications, 1990.

Twain, Mark. *The Innocents Abroad, or The New Pilgrims Progress.* New York: New American Library, 1980.

Uris, Jill, and Leon Uris. *Jerusalem.* New York: Doubleday, 1981.

Walker, Franklin. *Irreverent Pilgrims.* Seattle: University of Washington Press, 1974.

Williams, Albert N. *The Book by My Side.* New York: Duell, Sloan and Pearce, 1951.

Wurmbrand, Max. *The Jewish People.* London: Thames and Hudson, 1966.

Yadin, Yigael:
Bar-Kokhba. New York: Random House, 1971.
Hazor. New York: Random House, 1975.
Masada. New York: Random House, 1966.

PERIODICALS

Adler, Jerry, and Patrick Rogers. "The Unauthorized Dead Sea Scrolls." *Newsweek,* September 16, 1991.

Bahat, Dan. "Does the Holy Sepulchre Church Mark the Burial of Jesus?" *Biblical Archaeology Review,* May/June 1986.

Barkay, Gabriel:
"The Divine Name Found in Jerusalem." *Biblical Archaeology Review,* March/April 1983.
"The Garden Tomb—Was Jesus Buried Here?" *Biblical Archaeology Review,* March/April 1986.

Bull, Robert J. "Caesarea Maritima—The Search for Herod's City." *Biblical Archaeology Review,* May/June 1982.

Callaway, Joseph A. "Sir Flinders Petrie: Father of Palestinian Archaeology." *Biblical Archaeology Review,* November/December 1980.

Carmi, Israel. "How Old Is the Galilee Boat?" *Biblical Archaeology Review,* September/October 1988.

Cole, Dan. "How Water Tunnels Worked." *Biblical Archaeology Review*, March/April 1980.

Currid, John D. "Puzzling Public Buildings." *Biblical Archaeology Review*, January/February 1992.

"Dead Sea Doubts." *Scientific American*, June 1980.

Dothan, Trude, and Seymour Gitin. "Ekron of the Philistines." *Biblical Archaeology Review*, January/February 1990.

Fargo, Valerie M. "Sir Flinders Petrie." *Biblical Archaeologist*, December 1984.

Finkelstein, Israel. "Searching for Israelite Origins." *Biblical Archaeology Review*, September/October 1988.

Gitin, Seymour, and Trude Dothan. "The Rise and Fall of Ekron of the Philistines." *Biblical Archaeologist*, December 1987.

Hohlfelder, Robert L.:
"Caesarea beneath the Sea." *Biblical Archaeology Review*, May/June 1982.
"Herod the Great's City on the Sea: Caesarea Maritima." *National Geographic*, February 1987.

"Huntington Library Releases Scroll Photographs." *Biblical Archaeology Review*, November/December 1991.

King, Philip J. "Edward Robinson: Biblical Scholar." *Biblical Archaeologist*, December 1983.

Kloner, Amos, and Nahum Sagiv. "Maresha in the Shephcia: Olive-Oil Production in the Hellenistic Period." *Israel Land and Nature*, Winter 1989/90.

Mazar, Eilat. "Royal Gateway to Ancient Jerusalem Uncovered." *Biblical Archaeology Review*, May/June 1989.

Netzer, Ehud:
"Jewish Rebels Dig Strategic Tunnel System." *Biblical Archaeology Review*, July/August 1988.
"The Last Days and Hours at Masada." *Biblical Archaeology Review*, November/December 1991.
"Searching for Herod's Tomb." *Biblical Archaeology Review*, May/June 1983.

"The Newest of the Dead Sea Scrolls." *Time*, January 24, 1977.

Ostling, Richard N.:

"The Computer Keys' Scrolls." *Time*, September 16, 1991.
"Secrets of the Dead Sea Scrolls." *Time*, August 14, 1989.

Raban, Avner, and Robert R. Stieglitz. "The Sea Peoples and Their Contributions to Civilization." *Biblical Archaeology Review*, November/December 1991.

Ritmeyer, Kathleen, and Leen Ritmeyer. "Reconstructing Herod's Temple Mount in Jerusalem." *Biblical Archaeology Review*, November/December 1989.

Ross, Philip E. "Overview: Dead Sea Scrolls: Will Their Editors Perish before Publishing?" *Scientific American*, November 1990.

"Scholars Corner: New Analysis of the Crucified Man." *Biblical Archaeology Review*, November/December 1985.

Shanks, Hershel:
"The City of David after Five Years of Digging." *Biblical Archaeology Review*, November/December, 1985.
"Excavating in the Shadow of the Temple Mount." *Biblical Archaeology Review*, November/December 1986.
"Intrigue and the Scroll—Behind the Scenes of Israel's Acquisition of the Temple Scroll." *Biblical Archaeology Review*, November/December 1987.
"The Religious Message of the Bible" (Interview with Père Benoit). *Biblical Archaeology Review*, March/April 1986.

Sheler, Jeffrey L.:
"The Bible's Last Secrets: Deciphering the Mysterious Dead Sea Scrolls." *U.S. News & World Report*, October 7, 1991.
"Can Ideas Be Held Hostage?" *U.S. News & World Report*, June 25, 1990.

Shiloh, Yigal. "The Rediscovery of Warren's Shaft." *Biblical Archaeology Review*, July/August 1981.

Specter, Michael. "Library to Release Dead Sea Scrolls." *Washington Post*, September 22, 1991.

Stegemann, Hartmut. "Is the Temple Scroll a Sixth Book of the Torah—Lost for 2,500 Years?" *Biblical Archaeology Review*, November/December 1987.

Tzaferis, Vassilios. "Crucifixion—The Archaeological Evidence." *Biblical Archaeology Review*, January/February 1985.

Vann, Lindley. "News from the Field: Herod's Harbor Construction Recovered Underwater." *Biblical Archaeology Review*, May/June 1983.

Wachsmann, Shelley. "The Galilee Boat—2,000-Year-Old Hull Recovered Intact." *Biblical Archaeology Review*, September/October 1988.

Wood, Bryant G.:
"Did the Israelites Conquer Jericho?" *Biblical Archaeology Review*, March/April 1990.
"The Philistines Enter Canaan." *Biblical Archaeology Review*, November/December 1991.

Yadin, Yigael. "The Temple Scroll—The Longest and Most Recently Discovered Dead Sea Scroll." *Biblical Archaeology Review*, September/October 1984.

Zertal, Adam. "Following the Pottery Trail: Israel Enters Canaan." *Biblical Archaeology Review*, September/October 1991.

OTHER SOURCES

"Ashkelon Discovered: From Canaanites and Philistines to Romans and Moslems." Booklet. Washington, D.C.: Biblical Archaeology Society, 1991.

McCarter, P. Kyle, Jr. "The Mystery of the Copper Scroll." In *The Dead Sea Scrolls after Forty Years*. Proceedings of symposium at the Smithsonian Institution, October 27, 1990. Washington, D.C.: Biblical Archaeology Society, 1991.

"A Man and His Land: Highlights from the Moshe Dayan Collection." Catalog. Jerusalem: Israel Museum, 1986.

Shanks, Hershel. "The Excitement Lasts: An Overview. In *The Dead Sea Scrolls after Forty Years*. Proceedings of symposium at the Smithsonian Institution, October 27, 1990. Washington, D.C.: Biblical Archaeology Society, 1991.

"Treasures of the Holy Land: Ancient Art from the Israel Museum." Catalog. New York: Metropolitan Museum of Art, 1986.

Numerals in italics indicate an illustration of the subject mentioned.

A

Abel-Keramim: 56
Abraham: 16, 20, 44, 85, 158
Absalom's Tomb: *27*
Aegean: Iron Age technology of, 69; upheavals in, 68
Aelia Capitolina: 17
Ahab: 34, 46, 54
Aharoni, Yohanan: 64-65
Ain es Sultan: 63
Ains-shems: 22
Akhenaten: 64, 90
Akhziv: terra-cotta mask found at, *cover*
Albright, William Foxwell: 16, 36, 51, 54
Alexander the Great: 17, 80, 102, 159
Alt, Albrecht: 62, 65, 67
Amarna Letters: 64, *65*, 90
Amenhotep III: 90
American Institute of Holy Land Studies: 138
American Schools of Oriental Research (ASOR): 36, 111, 113
Ammonites: 56, 57; defeat of by King David, *72-73*
Anata: 20
Anathoth: 20
Andover Theological Seminary: 20
Andrew (apostle): 129
Annas: and arrest of Jesus, 139
Antiochus IV: 102, 159
Antonia Fortress: 101, 138
Antony, Mark: 144
Aphek, battle of: 71
Apiru: 64
Archaeological methods: artifacts, interpretation of (New Archaeology), 37; computer mapping, *55, 56;* ground-penetrating radar (GPR), 56, *57;* laser theodolites, use of, *55;* measuring devices used for, *55;* neutron activation analysis (NAA), 58; potsherd dating, 31-32; stratification, 64
Ark of the Covenant: 22, 70, *71,* 88, 90-91
Armageddon: 36
Artaxerxes: 101
Ashdod: 70, 90
Asherah (deity): 50; gold plaque of, *30*
Ashkelon: 70; bronze calf found at, *75;* excavations at, *75-83;* grave goods found at, 76, *77;* religious icons excavated from, *81;* Sanctuary of the Calf in, *76*
Assyrians: 22, 34, 54, 95, 158
Augustus Caesar: 46, 123, 144, 152
Avigad, Nahman: 91, 95, 98-99, 107-108, 143
Azekah: destruction of, 37

B

Baal Hamman (deity): 49
Babylonia: 80, 95, 98-100, 159; and destruction of the First Temple, 37, 137, 158
Baedeker, Karl: 30
Baigent, Michael: 116
Balfour, Lord: 34
Balfour Declaration: 34
Barclay, J. T.: 106
Barclay's Gate: 106-107
Barkay, Gabriel: 13-15, 99-100
Bar-Kokhba: and the Second Revolt, *134-135;* letters of, *135*
Bayt Sahur: excavations at, 124
Begin, Menachem: 51
Beirut: 20, 28
Beitin: 21-22
Benayahu: 98
Ben-Dov, Meir: 104, 106-107
Ben-Gurion, David: 134
Ben Yair, Eleazar: 132; ostraca marked for, 132, *133*
Bethar: 134
Bethel: 21-22
Bethlehem: 13, 18, 110, 111, 115, 124
Bethsaida: Peter's home at, 127-128
Beth-shan: clay sarcophagus found at, *35;* excavations at, 36
Beth-shemesh: 22; Ark of the Covenant returned to, *71*
Bible: 14, 19; dating for compilation of the Pentateuch, 59; and Dead Sea Scrolls, 113, 123; oldest known text from, *12,* 14-15; placenames in, correlation with modern sites, 21-22; as source of history and archaeological concerns, 16, 17, 33, 36-37, 123
Biran, Avraham: 122
Bliss, Frederick: 33
Breeden, Paul: art by, *end paper, 158-159*
Bullae (clay seals): *98-99*
Bultmann, Rudolf: 123
Burnt House: excavations at, *142, 143*
Burton, Sir Richard: 27
Byblos: 158
Byzantines: 75

C

Caesarea Maritima: 55, 138, 159; harbor complex at, *152-153;* inscriptions at, *123,* 125; Roman aqueduct at, *156-157;* storage vaults at, *154-155;* theater at, *155*
Caiaphas: and arrest of Jesus, 139
Cairo: 30, 33
Canaan: *map end paper;* alliances with Egypt, 64; cities of, 31, 41, 49, 52, 59, 67; Israelite settlement of, 50-51, 54-62, 64-67, 158; ivory cosmetic box, *66;* jewelry excavated from, *30;* Philistine settlements in, 69-74; survival of local religious tradition, 73; transition from Bronze Age to Iron Age, 54, 65-66, 67; village life in, 65-66; waning of Egyptian influence in, 70, 76, 90
Capernaum: 125; excavations at, 126-127, *128-129*
Cemeteries: archaeological analysis of, 119-120; dog cemetery excavated at Ashkelon, 80, *81;* in Jerusalem, 15, 119, *120,* 121-122
Chambord, Comte de: *29*
Church of the Holy Sepulcher: 44, *141;* relics from, 18
Church of the Nativity: 124, 128
Cohen, Orna: 136
Coins: found at Capernaum, 127; overstruck Roman coins issued by Bar-Kokhba, *135;* Phoenician, 80; use in establishing archaeological chronologies, 32
Constantine: 17, 18, 141
Convent of Saint Catherine: *39*
Cook, Thomas: guidebooks published by, *27, 30*
Corbo, Virgilio: 127-128
Crucifixion: archaeological evidence of, *120,* 121-122; and Jesus, 139-140
Cuneiform: and Amarna Letters, 64, *65;* inscriptions found at Tell el-Hesi, 33
Cyprus: trade with Ashkelon, 77
Cyrus: 100, 159

D

Dagon: Philistine temple at, 71
Damascus: 30, 52, 125
Danites: 58
David: 22, 27, 36, 43, 56, 57, *73,* 74, 78, 84, 98, 99, 124, 158; defeats Ammonites, *72-73;* and Jerusalem, 13, 85, 87, 90-92

Dayan, Moshe: archaeological interests of, 92, *93*
Dead Sea: *10-11,* 43, 61, 63, 109, 123, 134, 144
Dead Sea Scrolls: *109-117;* dates for, 14; display at Shrine of the Book, *117*
Deborah: 59
Decapolis: 125
De Forest, John William: 28
Delilah: 41
Department of Antiquities for Arab Palestine: 112
de Vaux, Roland: and Dead Sea Scrolls, 116, 117; excavations at Qumran complex, *112,* 113-114
Dever, William: 37
Dome of the Rock: 18, 26, *44-45,* 85, *86-87, 89,* 93
Donceel, Pauline: 117
Donceel, Robert: 117
Doré, Gustave: etching by, *72-73*
Dothan, Trude: 71
Dura-Europos: wall painting from, *71*

E

Edomites: 96, 104
Egeria: and house of Peter at Capernaum, 127-128
Eglon: 31, 32
Egypt: and Canaan, 33, 50, 70, 75, 76, 90, 158; development of civilization in, 16; evidence of Hebrew settlements in, 68; Petrie's archaeological work in, 30-31; and Philistine presence in Canaan, 68, 69-70; search for biblical sites in, 20, 21; trade routes to Damascus, 125
Ekron: excavations at, 70-71, 73; Philistine drinking cup recovered from, *68*
El (deity): Golden Calf of, *158*
Elijah: 85
En Gedi: *42-43*
Ennion: glassware fashioned by, 107-108
Eshkol, Levi: 115
Essenes: 113-114, 115, 116, 117, 123-124
Exodus: 17, 21, 65; dating for, 64; lack of archaeological evidence for, 54, 68; pharaoh, identification of, 32-33

F

Finkelstein, Israel: 67
First Jewish Revolt: 132, 144

Fisher, Clarence: 33
Flaubert, Gustave: 27, 28
Fleming, James: 138
Florus: on Herod's Temple, 105
Franciscans: archaeological activity by, 127-130

G

Galilee: *8-9,* 15, 123, 125, 137; excavations in, 49-50, 51; investigations by Robinson and Smith in, 24
Galilee, Sea of: 49, 125, 130, 137
Garstang, John: 63, 64, 75, 76, 82
Gath: 70
Gaza: *40-41,* 64, 70; Egyptian artifacts recovered at, 93; excavations at, 31
Gemaryahu: 98, 99
Geographic Information Systems (GIS): 56, 57
Gethsemane: 139
Gezer: excavations at, 33; gold-foil figurines found at, *34*
Gibraltar: 25
Gihon spring: *22, 25,* 95
Gitin, Seymour: 71
Giza: 30; excavations by Reisner at, 34
Golan Heights: 50
Golgotha: *140, 141,* 143
Goliath: 22, 74
Gordon, Charles: 143
Gottwald, Norman: 66-67, 68
Grave goods: 76, *77;* from excavations in Valley of Hinnom, 14, 99-100
Great Rift Valley: earthquakes in, 61
Greece: trade with Ashkelon, 81; two-handled cup made in, *81*
Green, Mr. (Harry Orlinsky): 112

H

Hadrian: 17, 134, 139, 141, 156
Haganah: 51
Haggai: 100
Harding, G. Lankester: *112*
Harvard University: 75
Hasmoneans: 102, 159
Hazor: 59, 64; Canaanite temple at, *50-51;* clay mask and potter's wheel excavated at, *48;* excavations by Yadin at, 49-50, *52, 53;* walls of, *53*
Hebrew: characters of the Tetragrammaton, 14; inscription at Hezekiah's tunnel, 24; linguistic connections with Aramaic and Arabic, 21

Hebrew Union College (Cincinnati): 116
Hebrew University: 111, 136
Helena: identification and commemoration of Holy Land sites, 18, 19, 124, 141, 143
Herod Antipas: 129
Herodium: Herod's palace complex at, *148-151*
Herod the Great: 26, 82, 119, 120, 124, 125, 129, 137, 159; and construction of Caesarea Maritima, *152-157;* palaces of, 138, *144-151;* reconstruction of the Temple, *101,* 104-106, 123, 144; as Roman puppet, 104, 123, 144; search for burial place of, 150
Hezekiah: 22, 95, 98
Hezekiah's tunnel: *22-23,* 24, *25*
Hiram: 92
Hohlfelder, Robert: 152
Holy Land: archaeological work in, spiritual dimensions of, 15-16; and Crusades, 18, 75, 82, 141; geographic boundaries of, 15-16; and 19th-century tourists, *27-29;* Roberts's lithographs of, 38, *39-47. See also* Canaan, Palestine
Holy Land, The (Roberts): 38; lithographs from, *39-47*
House of Kathros: 108
Hugo, Victor: 27
Huntington Library: 117
Hyksos: 76, 77, 158

I

Inscriptions: on bullae (clay seals), 98; at Caesarea Maritima, *123;* cuneiform, 33, 64, *65;* Hebrew, 24, 33, 37, 94; Hezekiah's tunnel, 24; Temple Mount stone, *105, 107;* use in establishing archaeological chronologies, 32
Institute of Nautical Archaeology (Texas A & M University): 131
Isaac: 44, 85
Isaiah: 22
Isaiah Scroll: *116,* 117
Israel: 16; establishment of modern Jewish state, 37, 111, 143; Six-Day War, 90, 115, 119; war of independence, 51
Israel Antiquities Authority: 96
Israel Department of Antiquities and Museums: 119, 122, 130
Israelites: 17, 74; Assyrian destruction of Samaria, 34; egalitarian and theocratic society of early Israelites, 68; establishment of pres-

ence in Canaan, 50-51, 54-62, 64-68, 76; and Philistines, 69, 70, 73-74, 78; pottery of, *67;* rift between Mosaic and Hellenistic Jews, 102; survival of in Jerusalem following Nebuchadnezzar's conquest, 99-100; transformation to monarchic society, 73-74, 158; use of Aramaic in daily life, 100

Israel Museum: 14, 93, 94

Israel stele: *32,* 54; discovery of at Thebes by Petrie, 32-33

J

Jacob: 13, 22

Jaffa: 30, 86, 88, 90

Jakoob esh-Shellaby: *24*

James (apostle): 129

Jebusites: 90

Jefferson, Thomas: 122

Jehoiakim: 98

Jeremiah: 20

Jericho: 17, 64; biblical narrative of fall of, 62-63; excavations at, *60-61, 62,* 89; ritual skulls recovered from, *63*

Jerusalem: *map inside front cover,* 15, 28, 30, 34, 74, 95, 101, 102, 141; Absalom's Tomb, *27;* Arch of Ecce Homo, *29, 118;* courtyard of Jesus' judgment, *139;* destruction of by Nebuchadnezzar, 37, 78, 85, 98-99, 158; destruction of by Romans, 17, 121, 125, *142, 143,* 159; excavations in, 89-90, 91, 95, 98, 119, *120,* 121-122, 136-137, *142, 143;* furnishings and mosaics of Herodian-era homes, *106-107,* 108; Golden Gate, 138; Hezekiah's tunnel, *22-24;* made Israelite capital by David, 13, 85, 87, 90-92; modern view of, *86-87;* Old City (Jewish Quarter), *86-87,* 89, 90, 107, 138, *141;* 19th-century environs of, *map* 20; Parker's search for Solomon's "hidden treasure," 86-88; pilgrims to, 18, 88, 106; plaque from ancient synagogue at, *136-137;* Pool of Bethesda, *126;* practical difficulties of excavating in, 88-89; reconstructed view of, 91, *95;* renamed Aelia Capitolina by Romans, 17; Roberts's lithograph of, *44-45;* terra-cotta figure found at, *84;* underground water supply system for, *cross-section diagram* 25, 95; Valley of Hinnom, 13, 99-100; Western Wall, *28*

Jerusalem School of ASOR: 36

Jesus of Nazareth: 13, 17, 18, 85; attempts to locate "historical" Jesus, 121-123; crucifixion and burial of, 121, 139-143; in Jerusalem, 119, 124, 125, 126, 137-143, 159; relics of, 18-19, 21, 122

Jewish Antiquities (Josephus): 104

Jewish War, The (Josephus): 104

Jews: burial practices and tombs of, 119, *120,* 121; enforced diaspora of, 143; messianic sects, 123-124; presence maintained by in Palestine, 18-19; rebellions against Rome, 121, *132-133, 134-135,* 143, 144. *See also* Israelites

John (apostle): 36, 125, 129

John Hyrcanus: 96

John Hyrcanus II: 102

John the Baptist: 129

Joppa: 64

Jordan: and Jerusalem's Old City, 90

Jordan River: *28,* 62, 63, 125

Joseph of Arimathea: 140-141

Josephus, Flavius: 82, 102, 104, 105, 107, 114, 121, 122, 136, 140, 150, 152, 155

Joshua: 31, 32, 37, 50, 51, 54, 59, 62-63, 64, 67

Joshua (son of high priest): and reconstruction of the Temple, 100

Josiah: 95

Judah (kingdom): 13; Babylonian conquest of, 37, 95, 98-100, 159

Judah Maccabee: 102, 159

Judas Iscariot: 139

Judea: client state of imperial Rome, 102-104, 159; Maccabean liberation of, 102; under Persian Empire, 100-101; Pilate as Roman governor of, 123, 137, 159; renamed Palestine by Romans, 17; and Second Revolt, 134

Judean Desert: *6-7,* 16, 18

Jupiter (deity): Romans dedicate Jerusalem to, 17

Justin Martyr: 124

Juvelius, Valter: 85-86

K

Kando: and the Dead Sea Scrolls, 110-112, *114,* 115

Kenyon, Kathleen: *63;* excavations at Jericho, 62, 63-64; excavations in Jerusalem, 89-90, 91, 94-95

Khalil, Sheik: 87, 88

Khirbet Ajlan: 31

Kidron Valley: 139

Kilburn, Benjamin: stereographs taken by, *28*

Kloner, Amos: 96

L

Lachish: 32, 37, 90, 95, *158;* searching for potsherds at, *36-37*

Lasers: archaeological uses of, 55

Lateran basilica (Rome): reputed relics held by, 19

Leigh, Richard: 116

Lemaire, André: 93-94

Leon Levy Expedition: excavations at Ashkelon, *75-83*

Linguistics: use in identification of biblical placenames, 21-22

Loffreda, Stanislao: 127-128

Lufhan, Moshe: 130

Lufhan, Yuval: 130

M

Macalister, Robert Alexander Stewart: 33

Maccabees: 96

Madaba Plains: 56

Magdala: 129. *See also* Migdal

Maison Bonfils: 28

Mansion, The: furnishings of Herodian-era home, 107-108

Maresha: excavation of Edomite settlement at, *96-97*

Marlborough, duchess of: 86

Marston, Sir Charles: 63

Martineau, Harriet: *27*

Mary (mother of James the Less): 141

Mary: relics of, 18, 19

Mary Magdalene: 129, 141

Mary's Well: 125

Masada: *144, 145;* burial cave at, *132-133;* defense of during First Jewish Revolt, 132, 159; Herod's palace fortress at, *144-147;* sandal and braided hair recovered at, *133*

Mazar, Benjamin: *104,* 106

Megiddo: 36, 90

Melville, Herman: 28

Mendenhall, G. E.: 65-66, 67, 68

Merenptah: mummy of, 32, *33;* traditional identification as pharaoh of the Exodus, 32

Merenptah stele: 54. *See also* Israel stele

Mesopotamia: and Canaan, 50; development of civilization in, 16

Metzger, Bruce: 122

Migdal: ancient fishing boat recovered at, *130-131;* excavations at,

129-131; mosaic from, 130, *131, 136*
Ministry of Housing (Israel): 119
Ministry of Tourism (Israel): 131
Mitannians: 64
Monastery of Saint Saba: *42-43*
Moses: 32, 34, 38, 50, 59, 75, 85, 158
Mosque of Omar: *See* Dome of the Rock
Mount Carmel: 155
Mount Gilboa, battle of: 73-74
Mount Moriah: 44, 93
Mount of Olives: 86
Mount Sinai: 21, *39,* 115
Muhammad: 16, 18, 44, 85, 88
Muhammad adh-Dhib: 109
Mycenae: 58, 78, 79

N

Nadelman, Yacov: *104*
Nazareth: 17, 125
Nebuchadnezzar: 37, 78, 98-99, 100, 158, 159
Negev Desert: 16, 92
Nehemiah: 101, 159
Neutron activation analysis (NAA): 58
Nike (deity): statue of, *82*
Numbers: biblical texts for, 14, 99

O

Omri: 33, 46
Ophel: 91; bullae (clay seals) uncovered at, *98-99;* excavations at, 88-89, 94-95, 98
Orfali, Gaudentius: 127
Orlinsky, Harry: 112
Osiris (deity): bronze figurine of, *81*
Ostheim, O. von: 28
Ostraca: recovered at Masada, 132, *133*
Ottoman Empire: 25, 26, 34; and control of Holy Land, 18, 86

P

Palestine: Arab and Jewish conflicts in, 34, 65; British political and academic interests in, 24-25, 34; derivation of name, 78; early Christian presence in, 18; and Egypt, 31; Islamic authority and foreign excavation in, 20, 26, 86; Islamic conquest of, 18; 19th-century topographical studies in, 21; reopening to scholarly research in 19th century, 19-20;

Romans rename province of Judea as, 17
Palestine Archaeological Museum: 112, 116
Palestine Exploration Fund (PEF): 24-26, 33, 126
Parker, Montague Brownslow: *88, 89;* and search for Solomon's "hidden treasure," 86-88
Paul: 159
Pentapolis (Five Cities of the Philistines): 41, 70, 78
Pentateuch: compilation of, 59
Persian Empire: and control of Holy Land, 80, 100, 159; decline of, 102; earring from, *159*
Petrie, Sir William Matthew Flinders: *30-31,* 37; discovery of Israel stele at Thebes, 32-33; excavations at Tell el-Hesi, 31, 32; pottery-based dating method developed by, 31-32, 36
Pharisees: 129, 137
Philistia: 78
Philistines: 17, 35, 73, 76, 158; ancient texts provide one-sided view of, 68; Ark of the Covenant captured by, 22, 70, 71; cities of, 41, 70, 75, 76, *78-79;* drinking cup (rhyton), *68;* feather headdress of, *35, 79;* iron weapons of, *69, 70, 71;* origins of, 68, 78, 79; pottery of, *69, 70, 71, 78, 79*
Philo of Alexandria: 137, 139
Phoenicians: 75, 80, 92, 93, 108, 158; terra-cotta mask, *cover*
Pilate, Pontius: 119, 137-138, 139, 140; inscription of, *123, 159*
Pliny: 114
Pomegranates: as decorative motif in Near Eastern art, *94, 158*
Pompey: 102, 159
Pool of Bethesda: *126*
Pool of Siloam: 22, *23*
Pottery: Israelite, *67;* neutron activation analysis of, 58, 71; Philistine, *69, 70, 71, 78, 79;* Phoenician, *81;* potsherds used to establish chronology, 31-32, 36, 52, 90, 120
Princeton Theological Seminary: 122
Ptolemies: 80, 102, 159

Q

Qumran: *cover;* cliff caves at, *110;* excavations of complex at, *112, 113,* 114, 123-124; ground plan of scriptorium, *113*

R

Radar: archaeological uses of, 56, *57*
Ramses II: 32, 93; identification as pharaoh of the Exodus, 33
Ramses III: 69-70, 79; relief carved for, *79*
Red Sea: 32, 33, 63
Reed, William: 113
Rehoboam: 158
Reisner, George: 33-34
Relics: Christian passion for, 18-19; silver bottles for consecrated oil, 18, *19;* spurious nature of, 19
Religion: archaeological research complicated by, 88-89; Canaanite cult figures, 63, 73, 75, 80, 94-95; Canaanite temple and furnishings, 49, *50-51;* child sacrifices conducted in Valley of Hinnom, 15; Christianity, growth of, 17-18, 143, 159; Christian pilgrimages to Holy Land sites, 18, *19,* 122; Christian relics, 18-19; Christian Scriptures and historical research, 122-123; Dead Sea Scrolls, 109, 113, 115-117; Essenes, 114, 115, 117, 123-124; healing cults, 80; as impetus for archaeological work in Holy Land, 15-16; Islamic connection to biblical prophets, 16; Islamic holy sites in Jerusalem, *89;* Jewish faith, Temple as embodiment of, 105-107; Jewish laws of ritual purity, 108; Yahweh cult, 65, 66, 68, 102
Rhyton: *68*
Roberts, David: *38;* lithographs of Holy Land by, *39-47*
Robinson, Edward: 30, 36, 102, 106; and Hezekiah's tunnel: 22-24, 26, 95; identification of sites in Palestine, 20-22, 24, 126
Robinson's Arch: *102-103,* 106
Roman Empire: and destruction of Herod's Temple, 104, 136, 159; and practice of crucifixion, 121, 139-140; rule in Holy Land, 17, 21, 75, 80, 82, 125, 132, 159
Royal Engineers (British): 25
Royal Stoa: 101

S

Saint Jerome: 122
Saint Lawrence chapel: reputed relics held by, 19
Saint Mark's monastery: 110, 111
Saladin: 82

Salem: 90. *See also* Jerusalem

Salim: 90

Samaria: investigations by Robinson and Smith in, 24

Samaria (city): 37, 158; excavations by Reisner and Fisher at, 33-34; ivory figurines found in, *34-35;* renamed Sebaste by Herod, 46; ruins at, *46-47*

Samson: 41

Samuel: 73

Samuel, Athanasius Yeshua: 110, 111, 112

Sanctuary of the Calf: *76*

Sargon: 95

Saul: 35, 36, 43, 73-74, 78, 158

Schiff, Jacob: 33

Schliemann, Heinrich: 31

Scrolls: biblical texts found in Valley of Hinnom, *12,* 14-15; Dead Sea Scrolls, *109-117;* techniques for unraveling of, 14-15, *114;* use of bullae with, *98-99*

Sea Peoples: 68, 79, 158

Sebaste: 46

Seilun: ancient placename for, 22

Seleucids: and rule in Holy Land, 80, 159

Sennacherib: 22, 95, 158

Sepphoris: 125

Severus: 82

Shahin, Khalil Iskander: *See* Kando

Shaphan: 98

Sheba, queen of: 92

Sheep Pool: *126*

Shemer: 33

Shenhav, Joseph: restoration of Dead Sea Scrolls, *114*

Shiloh (city): 22, 90

Shiloh, Yigal: 88-89, *90-91,* 98, 99

Shrine of the Book: *117*

Sicarii: 123, 144

Silva, Flavius: 132

Simon the Builder: ossuary of, 120-121

Six-Day War: 90, 115, 119

Smith, Eli: 20, 21, 24; and Hezekiah's tunnel, 22-24, 26

Solomon: 33, 54, 88, 99, 158; and Jerusalem's age of greatness, 92-93. *See also* Temple (Solomon)

Stager, Lawrence: 75, 76, 78, 79, 80

Stanhope, Lady Hester: 75

Starkey, John: 37

Steffy, J. Richard: 131, 136

Stegemann, Hartmut: 116

Sukenik, Eleazar: 111, 112

Syria: 34; and ancient Jerusalem, 90; Seleucid dynasty in, 102; trade with Ashkelon, 77

Syrian Desert: 16

T

Tacitus: on Herod's Temple, 105

Talmud: composition of, 18-19

Tamireh: 109, 110, 112, 113

Tanit (deity): bone cutout of, *81*

Tel Aviv: 152

Tel Aviv University: 13

Tel Dan: jar found at, *58*

Tell el-Ajjul: jewelry excavated from, *30*

Tell el-Amarna: 33; clay tablets discovered at, 64, *65*

Tell el-Hesi: 31-32, 33

Tell el-Umeiri: Ammonite fortifications at, 56, *57*

Tell Hum: 126

Tells: archaeological interest in, 31

Tel Miqne: 70-71

Temple (Herod): 25, 44, *101,* 104-106, 120-121, 125, 136, 138-139, 144; coin representing, *159;* destruction of, 104, 108, 121, 136

Temple (Solomon): 13, 14, 17, 25, 37, 44, 87, 89, 92-93, *95,* 99, 105; archaeological evidence of, 93, *94;* destruction of, 158; efforts for reconstruction, 100-101; reputed treasure hidden at, 85-86

Temple Mount: 25-26, 85, *86-87,* 91, *95,* 101, 102, 105, 106, 108, *124-125,* 138; inscribed stone from, *105,* 107

Temple of Dagon: 41

Temple Scroll: *114, 115,* 116

Tetragrammaton: 14

Thebes: excavation of Merenptah's tomb by Petrie, 32-33

Thenius, Otto: 143

Theodolites: *55*

Theodotos: inscribed plaque of, *136-137*

Tiberias: 131, 136

Tiberius: 123, 137

Tiryns: 58

Troy: Schliemann's excavations at, 31

Tushratta: 64

Tutankhamen: 90

Twain, Mark: 28

Tyropoeon Valley: 106

Tzaferis, Vassilios: 119-120, 124

U

Union Theological Seminary: 20

United Nations: 111

V

Vale of Elah: 22

Valley of Esdraelon: 59

Valley of Hinnom: 13, *14-15;* burial caves at, *12,* 14; scrolls found at, *12,* 14-15

Valley of the Slaughter: 15

Varus: 125

Vatican: and Dead Sea Scrolls, 116

Victoria: 25, 38

Vincent, Louis Hugues: 86-87

W

Wachsmann, Shelley: 130-137

Wadi Hasa: computer-generated maps of, *56;* excavations at, 56

Wadi Qumran: 109. *See also* Qumran

Wall Street Journal: advertisement for Dead Sea Scrolls, *111,* 112

Warren, Charles: *24,* 30; excavation of Jerusalem's underground water system, 25-30

Warren's Shaft: 26

Wilson, Charles: 126

Y

Yadin, Yigael: 51-52, 65; and Dead Sea Scrolls, 112, *114,* 115; excavations at Hazor, 49-50, 52-54; excavations at Masada, 132, 133, 144, *146-147;* letters of Bar-Kokhba, *134-135*

Yahtiri: 64

Yehohanan: crucifixion of, 121-122, 140

Yekutieli, Ruth: *114*

Z

Z, Mr.: and Dead Sea Scrolls, 114-115

Zealots: at Masada, 132, 133

Zerubbabel: reconstruction of the Temple, 100-101

Zionist movement: 34

Lake Huleh

Hazor

Capernaum

SEA OF
GALILEE

Migdal

STELE
WITH HANDS

PHILISTINE
SARCOPHAGUS

Beth-Shan

Nazareth

Tyre

Megiddo

N

AQUEDUCT

Caesarea

Athens

MEDITERRANEAN SEA

Babylon